PROOF THAT CHRISTIANS DO NOT DIE IN THE SEVEN YEAR GREAT TRIBULATION

Daniel Heynike

Copyright © 2025 by Daniel Heynike.

ISBN: 979-8-89465-119-4 (sc)
ISBN: 979-8-89465-120-0 (e)

All rights reserved. No part of this publication may be reproduced, distributed, or transmitted in any form or by any means, including photocopying, recording, or other electronic or mechanical methods, without the prior written permission of the author, except in the case of brief quotations embodied in critical reviews and certain other noncommercial uses permitted by copyright law.

Printed in the United States of America.

Integrity Publishing
39343 Harbor Hills Blvd Lady Lake,
FL 32159

www.integrity-publishing.com

DEDICATION

I have dedicated this book to Allan Ferguson who greatly encouraged me to write more books before he left Cape Town. He passed away on 7 Nov 2022 in Port Elizabeth, South Africa.

NOTES:

1: ALL QUOTES ARE FROM THE AUTHORIZED KING JAMES VERSION UNLESS OTHERWISE STATED
2: THIS EXPOSITION OF THE WORD IS WRITTEN FROM THE BORN-AGAIN CHRISTIANS POINT OF VIEW
3: THE QUOTATIONS FROM THE KING JAMES BIBLE ARE INFALLIBLE BUT THE REST IS MY INTERPRETATION OF THE WORD AND ENTIRELY FALLIBLE

CONTENTS

Foreword by the Author vii
Chapter 1:   The Overview 1
Chapter 2:   The Nature of God 3
Chapter 3:   The Seven-Year Tribulation Conflict Resolved. 4
Chapter 4:   What is Tribulation and Who is Causing it 7
Chapter 5:   Are there One or Two Second Comings. 11
Chapter 6:   How Do the Righteous Escape
                The Greatest Tribulation Ever 16
Chapter 7:   Looking for When the Rapture will Happen 21
Chapter 8:   My Understanding of Revelations 12. 24
Chapter 9:   The 1st 3.5 Years of the Antichrist's Rule 29
Chapter 10: My Understanding of the Christian Rapture 38
Chapter 11: The 2nd 3.5 Years of the Antichrist's Rule 55
Chapter 12: The 2nd Second Coming of the Lord at the End of
                The Greatest Tribulation Ever 61
Chapter 13: A Review of The Scripture's Professor Walter Veith
                Used to Make His Claim to Have Debunked the
                "Secret Rapture" 67
Chapter 14: The Final Conclusion of the Examination of
                Professor Walter Veith's Video Debunking the
                Secret Rapture 86
Annexure 1 A Complete Time Plot of The Last Days Events 87
Annexure 2 A Complete Time Plot of the Events in
                Revelations 12 88
Annexure 3: The Ark of The Covenant. .89
Books By The Same Author 91

FOREWORD BY THE AUTHOR

This book has come about because of a video published on YouTube by Professor Walter Veith titled "SECRET RAPTURE DEBUNKED". Although I have listened to many of Walter's sermons and gained immense understanding from them this alarmed me immediately as it meant that all living Christians would have to suffer the worst tribulation ever. So, I checked this teaching out with Jimmy Evans sermons, a man I trust, to find out he is in agreement with me that Christians do not go through greatest tribulation ever. You can listen to his YouTube debate titled "Rapture or No Rapture? The Great Debate: Jimmy Evans Uncovers the Signs of the Times!" for yourself.

I have written two books already on the End Times events, namely:

1. "THE GREAT END TIME DECEPTION EXPOSED" was written to contradict the popularly preached fallacy that all Christians would escape the seven-year great tribulation because they would be raptured first.
2. "REVELATIONS, AN EASY-TO-READ EXPLANATION OF JOHN'S REVELATION WITH TIMELINES FOR THE RAPTURE AND SECOND COMING" I wrote this to increase the awareness and understanding of THE END TIME prophecies in the Bible and to give an understanding of the prophesied order of events, including the Rapture.

So, with some confidence and much trepidation I decided to challenge Walter's interpretation. This book is the result of my investigations.

CHAPTER 1

THE OVERVIEW

Our first problem is that there is no single definitive scripture that conclusively proves a pre-great tribulation rapture. The weight of multiple scriptures will be needed. Next is Professor Walter Veith's title "SECRET RAPTURE DEBUNKED". Here he is saying that there will be no secret rapture before the second coming of Christ. This is correct, but not that it will not take place, but that it will not happen in secret. Scripture reveals that this event's timing will only be a secret until the trumpet bast (Matt 24:31) is heard throughout the world announcing it to all. So, the secrecy surrounding this event comes not only from not knowing when it will happen but also that it will be unexpected (Mark 13:32-33). We do not have to stay awake and pray all the time in order not to miss it as Jesus said one will be taken in his sleep and the other left (Luke 17v34). It is generally taught that we cannot know the day or time the rapture will take place but this is not entirely true as scripture shows that devout Christians will not be taken unawares (Luke 21v34). So, they will be aware of an imminent rapture before it happens. The teaching that there will not be a rapture before the second coming and the pervasive teaching that we cannot know the date and time of the rapture are both Satan's attempts to deceive Christians, leaving them unprepared for the worst event in history. Walter, by saying that there will be no rescue for Christians until Christ returns, is part of this deception by telling all living Christians they will have to suffer the worst tribulation ever till he returns. This will be a tribulation so intense that no person, animal or fish would have survived unless God in his compassion had not shortened its duration (Matt 24:21-22). This misinterpretation is not intentional but derives from the fact that he has not accepted that there will be two second comings of Christ. This I will discuss and prove later as I wish now to discuss the ramifications of his misinterpretation.

CHAPTER 2

THE NATURE OF GOD

God is good, God is love, God is faithful, God is long suffering, God is trust worthy, He will no desert those who put their faith in him, He is Holy and just, He is always the same. These are just some of the attributes the bible teaches about God. The bible is also full of stories of his defence and rescue of just men and women who have put their faith in him. So, without quoting hundreds of scripture verses confirming the above I am staggered to think that a highly esteemed bible teacher could even suggest that Jesus would just look on while all his living saints are tortured in the apocalypse. While this does happen to the two martyrs, no other saints are mentioned. This apparent sacrifice of all the saints who have been pardoned and washed in Christ's blood makes his sacrifice on the cross and their pardon seem futile. This does not reflect the Jesus I know and love to serve. Something must be wrong and I know what it is, it is the intertwined confusion that exists around the much repeated SEVEN-YEAR GREAT TRIBULATION and the timing(s) of second coming of Christ.

CHAPTER 3

THE SEVEN-YEAR TRIBULATION CONFLICT RESOLVED

As mentioned before, I wrote my first book "THE GREAT END TIME DECEPTION EXPOSED" to counter the common preaching that Christians would all escape the SEVEN-YEAR GREAT TRIBULATION because they would be raptured first. In this book I resolved the SEVEN-YEAR GREAT TRIBULATION controversy and produced an END TIMES TIME LINE up until the time of the rapture. Since then, I have produced a better time line which extends to the time of the NEW JERUSALEM for my second book, "REVELATIONS, an easy-to-read explanation of John's Revelation with timelines for the rapture and second coming". I wrote this last book to increase the awareness and understanding of the END TIME prophecies in the Bible and to give an understanding of the prophesied order of events, including the Rapture. I have included the last time line in the addendum as it is most helpful in understanding the sequence of all the events. In writing these two books I became aware that both my Minister and Professor Walter Veith, both which I greatly respect and admire, do not believe in a pre-tribulation rapture. This caused me great alarm and so I checked all my AUTHORIZED KING JAMES VERSION scriptures. They proved me to be correct which brought me to the conclusion that my interpretation could be a minority view. This is most alarming, if correct, as it could mean that most prophets and ministers are teaching that all Christians will have to survive the almost un-survivable "GREATEST TRIBULATION EVER" of which Jesus said "except those days should be shortened, there should no flesh be saved" (Matt 24: 22). This is a most horrific scenario as it means either home free or imminent destruction. The confusion around the SEVEN-YEAR GREAT TRIBULATION arises from misquotations from Daniel's peace deal prophesy.

This is Daniel's prophesy: Dan 9:27 "And he shall confirm the covenant with many for one week: and in the midst of the week he shall cause the sacrifice and the oblation to cease, and for the overspreading of abominations he shall make it desolate, even until the consummation, and that determined shall be poured upon the desolate."

Daniel, talking about the Antichrist, says he will make a week (7-year) peace treaty with Israel to allow Israel to build their 3rd Jewish temple in Jerusalem, in which the Antichrist secretly plans to sit and declare himself to be God. The 7-year peace treaty is terminated half way or after 3.5 years or 1260 days by the antichrist. "the overspreading of abominations he shall make it desolate" refers to Matt 24:15 "When ye therefore shall see the abomination of desolation, spoken of by Daniel the prophet, stand in the holy place,". The Antichrist's idol will be an abomination and desolate the temple. This prophesy is not very clear and can only be understood when combined with the other prophesies. Now the GREAT TRIBULATION is not mentioned in the book of Daniel but comes from Matt 24:3 when Jesus had just come from the temple and spoke about this time. Matt 24:3 "And as he sat upon the mount of Olives, the disciples came unto him privately, saying, Tell us, when shall these things be? and what shall be the sign of thy coming, and of the end of the world?" And he replied among other things: Matt 24:15 "When ye therefore shall see the abomination of desolation, spoken of by Daniel the prophet, stand in the holy place...... 21 For then shall be great tribulation, such as was not since the beginning of the world to this time, no, nor ever shall be." So, we know that halfway into the covenant (peace treaty) the worst tribulation, referred to in this book as THE GREATEST TRIBULATION EVER, will start and continue till Jesus comes again about 3.5 years later (see time line). So why does everyone refer to this tribulation as the SEVEN-YEAR GREAT TRIBULATION? It is a confliction of the 7 years of the Antichrist's reign till Jesus comes again and the 7 years of the peace treaty he signed. Here there is a paradox in that this is all a period of terrible trouble referred to as tribulation. The Antichrist will start his reign with the signing of a peace treaty which he makes with Israel but not with the Christians and the rest of the world. Rev 13:15 "And he had power to give life unto the image of the beast, that the image of the beast should both speak, and cause that as many as would not worship the image of the beast should be killed". Then just before the middle of the peace treaty and before he has killed all the Christians, the rapture takes place saving the saints. After this the Antichrist sits in the Jewish temple as god and turns on the Jews. This is the time all Jews are told to escape and head for the hills and hide till Jesus comes about 3.5 years later, to avoid the wrath of God, as be devastates the earth and the wrath of the Antichrist as he tries to kill all God's Jewish children. Matt 24:16 "Then let them which be in Judaea flee into the mountains". As you can see, there will 2 periods of 3.5 years, or 7 years of continual tribulation. This is why no one contradicts this period being called the Seven Year Tribulation. This is not yet the end of this story, but as we will see later, it is crucial for the understanding of the rapture that we understand who is doing what and who is in control.

Conclusion: There is a 7-year time of great tribulation beginning at the time of the Antichrist but only a 3.5-year GREATEST EVER TRIBULATION, called the WRATH OF GOD for the second half of his reign.

CHAPTER 4

WHAT IS TRIBULATION AND WHO IS CAUSING IT

What is tribulation?

Christianity.com defines it as: "tribulation means distress or suffering resulting from oppression or persecution". Similarly, Webster defines it as: distress or suffering resulting from oppression or persecution. Tribulation can therefore be a consequence of disobedience to God or the persecution of God's followers by satanically inspired people.

Concerning man-made tribulation:

When Adam and Eve disobeyed God, death entered the world and with it thorns, toil and disease. When God's authority was rejected, Satan took over the earth and his plan has always been the same, to deceive, destroy and kill. "And the great dragon was cast out, that old serpent, called the Devil, and Satan, which deceiveth the whole world: he was cast out into the earth, and his angels were cast out with him." Rev 12:9. Now consider that less than 30% of all peoples call themselves Christians (Google) and of these I estimate less than 10% are born again and living a life pleasing to God. So about 90% of all the above are serving or following Satan to some extent. Some slightly, with some others being all out satanists. They are in control of the world and are in it for personal honour and gain with little knowledge or regard to the outcome. They are destroying the earth and peoples of the earth with their wars and conflicts. This is the tribulation on the earth where people suffer because of men inspired by Satan. The ultimate example of this is the days before the apocalypse when the Antichrist and the false prophet gain power over all the world.

> "7 And it was given unto him to make war with the saints, and to overcome them: and power was given him over all kindreds, and tongues, and nations.
>
> 8 And all that dwell upon the earth shall worship him, whose names are not written in the book of life of the Lamb slain from the foundation of the world." Rev 13:7-8.

This is the time where it is as bad as man-made tribulation gets, for it is the time Christians can neither buy or sell. "16 And he causeth all, both small and great, rich and poor, free and bond, to receive a mark in their right hand, or in their foreheads: 17 And that no man might buy or sell, save he that had the mark, or the name of the beast, or the number of his name." Rev 13:16-17

Concerning God made tribulation:

There is also God made tribulation. A good example is Noah's flood when God saved 8 people and destroyed the rest. We will now discern if the "GREATEST TRIBULATION EVER" is caused by God or man. "And the nations were angry, and thy wrath is come, and the time of the dead, that they should be judged, and that thou shouldest give reward unto thy servants the prophets, and to the saints, and them that fear thy name, small and great; and shouldest destroy them which destroy the earth." Rev 11:18

This is a last day's prophecy in Revelations when God is about to release the "GREATEST TRIBULATION EVER" and destroy those who destroyed his earth. So, we can see that this final great event is the day of God's Judgement on the whole world and is the final result of man's wickedness. Now hope is given to the saints by the lord in 2 Peter 2:9. "The Lord knoweth how to deliver the godly out of temptations, and to reserve the unjust unto the day of judgment to be punished" In both the scriptures quoted above a distinction is made between the godly and the unjust indicating different destinations or an escape for the righteous.

Can the righteous escape the greatest tribulation ever?

We see that God is for us and has no desire for any of us to perish and says so in 2 Peter 3:9: "The Lord is not slack concerning his promise, as some men count slackness; but is longsuffering to us-ward, not willing that any should perish, but that all should come to repentance." Can we conclude that he will come to our help somehow from 1 Cor 10:13: "There hath no temptation taken you but such as is common to man: but God is faithful, who will not suffer you to be tempted above that ye are able; but will with the temptation also make a way to escape, that ye may be able to bear it."

The following scriptures display Jesus's nature:

> 4 "Surely he hath borne our griefs, and carried our sorrows: yet we did esteem him stricken, smitten of God, and afflicted.
>
> 5 But he was wounded for our transgressions, he was bruised for our iniquities: the chastisement of our peace was upon him; and with his stripes we are healed." Isa 53:4-5.

Here we see that Jesus died deliberately to take pain and punishment we deserved upon himself. This makes the death and sacrifice of Jesus to have been made in vain if God still needs to punish us for our offences together with the sinners in the last days of his vengeance. However, the best scripture that indicates that believers do not suffer the Greatest Tribulation Ever is 1 Thess 5:9-10:

9 For God hath not appointed us to wrath, but to obtain salvation by our Lord Jesus Christ,

10 Who died for us, that, whether we wake or sleep, we should live together with him.

The plan and purpose of God for Jesus and us

God the Father sent Jesus his son to die for us in our place and in so doing remove our sin so we could once more enter into the presence of the father and have fellowship with him. Considering that Jesus died a very terrible death for us on a cross to save us from the death penalty of our own sins, Jesus's death on the cross becomes pointless if we still have to be punished for our sins with the God haters, when he destroys those who destroyed his earth in the GREATEST TRIBULATION EVER. For the redeemed to go through this, the greatest tribulation ever, therefore contradicts the nature and purposes of God and He will therefore make a way of escape as he promised in 1 Cor 10:13 mentioned above. We now see why we need to know who is causing the tribulation, because if it is God he will make a way of escape for his saints. I am now satisfied that believers do not go through THE GREATEST TRIBULATION EVER but still have to find out the way of their escape.

CHAPTER 5

ARE THERE ONE OR TWO SECOND COMINGS

As explained earlier, my pastor and Professor Walter Veith do not agree that there are two second comings of Christ. This is critical because if he only comes once and at the end of the 3.5-year GREATEST TRIBULATION EVER, all those entering this time, including Jews and Christians, will have a very low survival expectancy. I believe in the two second comings because I cannot believe the forgiven saints will be put through this test. The two second comings happens if Jesus returns to collect his saints prior to or during the GREATEST TRIBULATION EVER and then returns again at the end of this tribulation. We will now examine both these theories in detail to see which one stands up to scrutiny.

The single second coming of Christ (interpretation 1)

In the single second coming of Christ everyone including the church go through the 3.5 year "greatest tribulation ever" prior to the rapture when Jesus gathers all of the saints, alive and dead, to meet him in the clouds before he reaches the earth. Jesus then descends to the earth, destroys the armies of Satan, binds Satan and then the marriage supper of the Lamb takes place on the earth.

The two second comings of Christ (interpretation 2)

In the two second comings of Christ, the saints are raptured before or during the 3.5 year "greatest tribulation ever" and all the rest, including the Jews, go through it. After being raptured Jesus takes the saints (church) to heaven to enjoy the marriage supper of the Lamb. After the 3.5 year "greatest tribulation ever" has taken place, he appears in the sky with the resurrected church and the angels and every eye sees him. He destroys the armies of Satan, binds Satan and then descends to the earth and his feet touch the Mount of Olives which splits in two.

Does the Word support interpretation 1 or 2

1. The nature of Christ

Here the very nature of Christ is clear proof that Interpretation 2 is correct since the Bible tells us that Jesus never physically hurt, condemned, punished or tempted anyone while He was on earth. It also tells us He is will not change but is the same forever. (Heb 13:8 Jesus Christ the same yesterday, and today, and for ever.)

2. Concerning hurt

In the Garden of Gethsemane, he did not attack or physically resist those arresting him. "And Jesus said unto him, Friend, wherefore art thou come? Then came they, and laid hands-on Jesus, and took him." Matt 26:50

3. Concerning condemning

"Verily, verily, I say unto you, He that heareth my word, and believeth on him that sent me, hath everlasting life, and shall not come into condemnation; but is passed from death unto life." John 5:24. "But when we are judged, we are chastened of the Lord, that we should not be condemned with the world." 1 Cor 11:32 The lady caught in adultery was released by Jesus without condemnation. "She said, No man, Lord. And Jesus said unto her, Neither do I condemn thee: go, and sin no more." John 8:11.

4. **Concerning punishment:**

'And to wait for his Son from heaven, whom he raised from the dead, even Jesus, which delivered us from the wrath to come." 1 Thess 1:10 We will be delivered from the wrath to come. The righteous go into life eternal life and not punishment: "And these shall go away into everlasting punishment: but the righteous into life eternal." Matt 25:46. So if punishment is reserved for the unrighteous how can the righteous saints be punished in the Greatest Tribulation Ever?

5. **Concerning temptation:**

"Because thou hast kept the word of my patience, I also will keep thee from the hour of temptation, which shall come upon all the world, to try them that dwell upon the earth" Rev 3:10 "There hath no temptation taken you but such as is common to man: but God is faithful, who will not suffer you to be tempted above that ye are able; but will with the temptation also make a way to escape, that ye may be able to bear it." 1 Cor 10:13. So, all are tempted to sin but God promises to help us escape sin. But God himself tempts no man. "Let no man say when he is tempted, I am tempted of God: for God cannot be tempted with evil, neither tempteth he any man" James 1:13.

Let us now look at the worst temptation I know off, that of Job, to see who does the tempting. Job feared (loved) God and had been hugely blessed by God. When God pointed out to Satan how wonderful and righteous Job was, Satan Replied:

> 9 "Then Satan answered the Lord, and said, Doth Job fear God for nought?
>
> 10 Hast not thou made an hedge about him, and about his house, and about all that he hath on every side? thou hast blessed the work of his hands, and his substance is increased in the land.
>
> 11 But put forth thine hand now, and touch all that he hath, and he will curse thee to thy face." Job 1:9-11

We see here God has both the power to stop and allow people to be tempted. God replies:

12 "And the Lord said unto Satan, Behold, all that he hath is in thy power; only upon himself put not forth thine hand. So Satan went forth from the presence of the Lord." Job 1:12

The consequence of this was that Job lost everything except his wife, who turned against him, but he remained faithful to God. Afterwards God restored his family and doubled his wealth.

Job 42:10 "And the Lord turned the captivity of Job, when he prayed for his friends: also the Lord gave Job twice as much as he had before."

So, it is Satan who tempts everyone and not the Lord Jesus.

6. **Concerning sin:**
"For the wages of sin is death; but the gift of God is eternal life through Jesus Christ our Lord." Rom 6:23. So the ultimate consequence of sin is death, but for those saved by faith in Jesus, it is eternal life.

7. **Concerning escape:**
"Watch ye therefore, and pray always, that ye may be accounted worthy to escape all these things that shall come to pass, and to stand before the Son of man." Luke 21:36

Conclusion of what does the Word support?

Judging by all the scriptures discussed above it seems very unlikely that God wishes all his saints to go through His great end time judgement when he punishes all those who destroyed his earth, also called the apocalypse. Rev 11:18 "And the nations were angry, and thy wrath is come, and the time of the dead, that they should be judged, and that thou shouldest give reward unto thy servants the prophets, and to the saints, and them that fear thy name, small and great; and shouldest destroy them which destroy the earth." I only know of two of his saints who will definitely go through the apocalypse, his two witnesses. "And I will give power unto my two witnesses, and they shall prophesy a thousand two hundred and threescore days, clothed in sackcloth." Rev 11:3. This all points to Interpretation 2, the two second comings of Christ as being correct but is not conclusive. It seems that only the determination of the timing of the rapture will solve the issue. So, we will examine each theory in more detail to see if we can find any evidence for either being correct.

CHAPTER 6

HOW DO THE RIGHTEOUS ESCAPE THE GREATEST TRIBULATION EVER

Because Interpretation 1, which we now believe to be false but have not yet proven so, is based on a single second coming, we will have to show that there are not one but two second comings. The one second coming version says that the rapture and the second coming are one and the same event as we are raptured to meet the Lord in the clouds and then immediately return to the earth for the marriage supper of the Lamb on earth. If I can show this last version to be erroneous the 2 comings version will be established as correct. It seemed obvious that because it is commonly known that we are coming back from heaven with the Lord riding on white horses, that the single coming must be incorrect. It is however not that easy as the word does not explicitly say the saints are coming back with the Lord. In 1 Thess 3v13, it says "To the end he may stablish your hearts unblameable in holiness before God, even our Father, at the coming of our Lord Jesus Christ with all his saints", which confirms we do come back with the Lord, but does not say from where. And in Zech 14v5 "And ye shall flee to the valley of the mountains; for the valley of the mountains shall reach unto Azal: yea, ye shall flee, like as ye fled from before the earthquake in the days of Uzziah king of Judah: and the Lord my God shall come, and all the saints with thee" it says we come back with the Lord but again does not say where from. In Rev 19v11-14 (below) we see Jesus coming on a white horse and his armies from heaven followed him on white horses. Again inconclusive.

> 11 "And I saw heaven opened, and behold a white horse; and he that sat upon him was called Faithful and True, and in righteousness he doth judge and make war.
>
> 12 His eyes were as a flame of fire, and on his head were many crowns; and he had a name written, that no man knew, but he himself.
>
> 13 And he was clothed with a vesture dipped in blood: and his name is called The Word of God.
>
> 14 And the armies which were in heaven followed him upon white horses, clothed in fine linen, white and clean."

The scriptures above do not disprove a 2nd second coming but do not confirm it either. This is not helping so we will try something else. In Rev 7v9-17 we are given a glimpse into heaven and see the following:

> "9 After this I beheld, and, lo, a great multitude, which no man could number, of all nations, and kindreds, and people, and tongues, stood before the throne, and before the Lamb, clothed with white robes, and palms in their hands;
>
> 10 And cried with a loud voice, saying, Salvation to our God which sitteth upon the throne, and unto the Lamb.
>
> 11 And all the angels stood round about the throne, and about the elders and the four beasts, and fell

before the throne on their faces, and worshipped God,

12 Saying, Amen: Blessing, and glory, and wisdom, and thanksgiving, and honour, and power, and might, be unto our God for ever and ever. Amen.

13 And one of the elders answered, saying unto me, What are these which are arrayed in white robes? and whence came they?

14 And I said unto him, Sir, thou knowest. And he said to me, These are they which came out of great tribulation, and have washed their robes, and made them white in the blood of the Lamb.

15 Therefore are they before the throne of God, and serve him day and night in his temple: and he that sitteth on the throne shall dwell among them.

16 They shall hunger no more, neither thirst any more; neither shall the sun light on them, nor any heat.

17 For the Lamb which is in the midst of the throne shall feed them, and shall lead them unto living fountains of waters: and God shall wipe away all tears from their eyes."

In verse 9 a great multitude which no man could number stood before the throne in heaven worshipping God. In verse 13 an elder asked John who they were and where they came from. He replied that the elder knew and was told that they had come out of great tribulation and washed their robes white in the blood of the Lamb. These are therefore the saints which have been redeemed from the earth, but they are in heaven and not on the earth. How did they get to heaven if after being raptured and meeting Jesus in the air they were returned straight back to the earth? This should conclusively prove that the Lord comes twice, but there is a problem. In verse 14 above is says: "These are they which came out of **great tribulation**". This general tribulation reading is crucial as it means that all the believers who ever suffered for Jesus are there. Because it is general It also does not indicate that they came out of a particular Great Tribulation called the **Greatest Tribulation Ever**. While this seems to prove the 2 comings version, it is entirely based on the King James Version.

Which rendering is correct?

Looking into this problem, I found that some versions confirm the KJV but others do not. Further researching this problem, I found that only the following versions had the same reading as the King James Version, the Douay-Rheims and Webster. Which is now the correct reading? I have reasoned as follows:

1. This event is the only recorded occasion in heaven that all the redeemed are found standing together in heaven before their Lord.
2. If these are only those coming out of the (about 3 ½ year) Greatest Tribulation Ever, where are the rest of the redeemed?
3. The number given, "a great multitude, which no man could number" does not correlate with a maximum of earths possible 2 billion current inhabitants.

I have therefore to conclude that the raptured believers are in heaven and are not described as having come out of **The Greatest Tribulation Ever**. Just the fact that we can confirm that saints have reached heaven also confirms the two second coming version is correct.

This controversy is now solved

The one second coming cannot be correct as he has to collect the believers and take them to heaven before returning triumphantly with them. This conclusively proves that the Lord returns twice. I am very pleased with this outcome. If I was wrong, we would have to go through the worst ever tribulation as the Lord would then only return after the tribulation. See Matt 24:29-30 below:

"29 Immediately after the tribulation of those days shall the sun be darkened, and the moon shall not give her light, and the stars shall fall from heaven, and the powers of the heavens shall be shaken:

30 And then shall appear the sign of the Son of man in heaven: and then shall all the tribes of the earth mourn, and they shall see the Son of man coming in the clouds of heaven with power and great glory."

Now that we know that the Rapture does occur, we only need to find out when it happens, to confirm that believers will not be raptured in the middle of the worst ever tribulation and still suffer tribulation.

CHAPTER 7

LOOKING FOR WHEN THE RAPTURE WILL HAPPEN

1st 3.5 years of the antichrist's rule. This period includes tribulations and the erection of the idol called the abomination of desolation

To avoid confusion, I will take a quick look at the two end time Jerusalem wars, but will only describe them in detail in their chronological places. The first war is called the Armageddon war because it takes place in the valley of Jezreel where the city of Megiddo was located on a hill. The hill of Megiddo is called Har-megiddo in Hebrew and Armageddon is a corruption of the name Har-megiddo. In Rev 16 verses 13-16 (see below) the false prophet, Armageddon and the rapture ("watcheth" refers to waiting for the rapture) are mentioned together indicating that this happens in the period of the antichrist.

Rev 16

> "13 And I saw three unclean spirits like frogs come out of the mouth of the dragon, and out of the mouth of the beast, and out of the mouth of the false prophet.
>
> 14 For they are the spirits of devils, working miracles, which go forth unto the kings of the earth and of the

whole world, to gather them to the battle of that great day of God Almighty.

15 Behold, I come as a thief. Blessed is he that watcheth, and keepeth his garments, lest he walk naked, and they see his shame.

16 And he gathered them together into a place called in the Hebrew tongue Armageddon."

The second end time Jerusalem war is called the Gog and Magog war. In Rev 20 (see below) we are told that after Christ's 1000-year reign, Satan will be released from the bottomless pit and bring all the nations together with Gog and Magog for battle and surround the beloved city Jerusalem. So, the Gog and Magog war happens at the end of the millennium, just before the Great White Throne Judgement.

Rev 20

"6 Blessed and holy is he that hath part in the first resurrection: on such the second death hath no power, but they shall be priests of God and of Christ, and shall reign with him a thousand years.

7 And when the thousand years are expired, Satan shall be loosed out of his prison,

8 And shall go out to deceive the nations which are in the four quarters of the earth, Gog and Magog, to gather them together to battle: the number of whom is as the sand of the sea.

9 And they went up on the breadth of the earth, and compassed the camp of the saints about, and the beloved city: and fire came down from God out of heaven, and devoured them."

The 1st 3.5 years of the antichrist's rule is revealed in Revelation Chapter 12. To help understand the events derived from this chapter I have added "My understanding of Revelations 12" from my book "Revelations" below:

CHAPTER 8

MY UNDERSTANDING OF REVELATIONS 12

Verse 1:
    Here we see a woman surrounded with the glory of God and the moon under her feet indicating a heavenly point of view. The crown of 12 stars indicates she is the origin of the 12 tribes of Israel or the 12 apostles or both. We conclude that she is both Israel and the Church of Christ.

Verse 2:
    This is a picture of Mary giving birth to Jesus, but also Israel giving birth to its Messiah and the church.

Verse 3:
    The red dragon is explained in verse 9 as "that old serpent, called the Devil, and Satan, which deceived the whole world". It has 7 heads and 7 crowns. As 7 is the number of God, it indicates that he intends to supplant God. The 7 heads with 7 crowns are 7 political and religious organizations that rule on the earth under his control. The 10 horns are the 10 puppet kings mentioned in Daniel 7 v24 that they will raise up.

Verse 4:
    When Satan was thrown out of heaven and down to the earth, he took one third of the angels with him. Satan planned to kill Jesus

and thereby destroy the Church before it was even born by getting king Herod to kill all the Bethlehem babies and thereby Jesus as well. See Matthew2v13

Verse 5:
This was Jesus who will reign with a rod of iron in the millennium (See Rev 19v15). After Jesus was raised from the dead, he ascended into heaven and sat down on the right hand of God in heaven (See Heb 10v12).

Verse 6:
Daniel in chapter 9v27 prophesied that the antichrist will make a 7-year peace treaty with Israel. This allows Israel to build their new Jewish temple in Jerusalem in which the antichrist secretly wants to sit and declare himself to be God, and so now changes his attention to persecuting the church and not Israel. The 7-year peace treaty is terminated after 3.5 years or 1260 days by the antichrist "In the midst of the week he shall cause the sacrifice and the oblation to cease, and for the overspreading of abominations he shall make it desolate". So, in the middle of the 7 years, that is after 1260 days, he will stop the sacrifice in the new Jewish temple and erect in it an idol called the abomination of desolation. This is what Jesus warned about in Matt 24:15&16 when he said "When ye therefore shall see the abomination of desolation, spoken of by Daniel the prophet, stand in the holy place, then let them which be in Judaea flee into the mountains". And Matt 24v21: "For then shall be great tribulation, such as was not since the beginning of the world to this time, no, nor ever shall be." This is the beginning of God's judgement on the earth to "destroy them that destroy the earth" (Rev 11v18). The born-again Christians are raptured before this time because of 1 Thess 5v9&10 which says "For God hath not appointed us to wrath, but to obtain salvation by our Lord Jesus Christ, Who died for us, that, whether we wake or sleep, we should live together with him". Verse 6 reveals that the Jews will be helped by the Holy Spirit to escape from the antichrist because he will be restrained from entering Edom, Moab and part of Ammon. In Dan 11v41 we read "He shall enter also into the glorious land, and many countries shall be overthrown: but these shall escape out of his hand, even Edom, and Moab, and the chief of the children

of Ammon." So, they will also be sheltered and fed for 3.5 years or 1260 days and so avoid the coming anger and retribution of God. We assume that the 1260 days marks the end of the greatest tribulation ever period but Daniel refers to a longer period of 1290 days in Dan 12v11: "And from the time that the daily sacrifice shall be taken away, and the abomination that maketh desolate set up, there shall be a thousand two hundred and ninety days" Daniel also refers to a longer period of 1335 days that will be a blessing. Dan 12:12 "Blessed is he that waiteth, and cometh to the thousand three hundred and five and thirty days."

This last scripture, I assume, is the day of the Lord's return. (See timeline in annexure 2)

Verse 7 to 9:

In Luke 10:18 Jesus said "And he said unto them, I beheld Satan as lightning fall from heaven." Also, Rev 12v13 confirm Satan being cast down at the time of the rapture when he and his angels are judged. These verses are a full account of the event.

Verse 10 & 11:

These 2 verses taken together announce the final and ultimate triumph of good over evil. The saints are in heaven having overcome Satan by the blood of the Lamb, their testimony and being willing to die for their Lord.

Verse 12:

There is now great rejoicing in heaven as the righteous are all there, celebrating after being raptured, but on earth God is pouring out his wrath, for the great day of the Lord has come. Satan has now lost his chief victim, the church, as he can no longer accuse them when he is on earth and they are in heaven. He is very angry.

Verse 13:

The only victims left now for Satan to persecute are his own people, the non-believers, so he chooses to persecute Gods non-believing children, the non-believing Jews.

Verse 14:

The explanation of verse 6 explains this, except for the "time, and times, and half a time" which is 1 year, 2 years and half a year or the 3.5 years or the 1260 days the Jews are sheltered from the antichrist.

Verse 15:

This verse has been very difficult to interpret and I only have an idea about it so I will rather talk about it in the commentary section on the antichrist than here.

Verse 16:

I will explain this also in the commentary section as it is connected.

Verse 17:

This verse has been the most difficult of all to interpret. The reference to "her seed, which keep the commandments of God, and have the testimony of Jesus Christ" caused me to think that I had got the timing of the rapture wrong as this seemed to indicated that born-again Christians were still on the earth. The only ones that I could think maybe there were the two witnesses. Rev 11:3 says "And I will give power unto my two witnesses, and they shall prophesy a thousand two hundred and threescore days". This period could refer to the first 3.5 year of the peace treaty before it is cancelled or the same period after it of 3.5 years that the woman is protected. (See Rev 12 verse 6). Now Rev 11:13-15 tells us that in the same hour that the two witnesses were raised up to heaven there was a great earthquake which destroyed a tenth of Jerusalem. Just after this we are told in verse 15 that Christ has begun to reign over all the earth forever. God gave Adam dominion over all he had created in Gen 1v28-29 and then he lost it to Satan when he sinned. So, judgement began as Christ took back rulership of all the earth from Satan, immediately after the two witnesses finished their witnessing. Hence the 3.5 years referred to in Rev 11 verse 3 has to be during the entire duration of the peace treaty prior to the erection of an idol called the abomination of desolation in the new Jewish temple leading to God's outpouring of wrath on the Day of the Lord.

So here is what I think verse 17 is saying: The woman here is both Israel and the Church. And now the only ones left for Satan to avenge himself on, are the remaining Jews and the remaining unsaved Christians. He is after the remaining secular Christians because they have acknowledged that Jesus died for them and claim to be Christians, but still have not yet given their lives to Christ and do not cooperate with the antichrist.

CHAPTER 9

THE 1ST 3.5 YEARS OF THE ANTICHRIST'S RULE

The time of the antichrist starts with a peace treaty, the two witnesses and allows the 3RD Jewish temple to be built

We now come to the time of the antichrist who rules for a little more than 7 years.

The prophet Daniel informs us in Dan 9:27 "And he shall confirm the covenant with many for one week", from this we understand that the antichrist will establish a 7-year peace covenant with Israel. This is the first appearance of the antichrist that we know of. From here things move fast and all the scripture references, from all over the Bible can get very confusing. A good look at ANNEXURE 1, A COMPLETE TIME PLOT OF THE LAST DAYS EVENTS, will show you the sequence of events from before the antichrist to the new Jerusalem. Understanding the order of events will give you an overview of the last days.

I will now focus on the time of the antichrist. A good look at ANNEXURE 2, A COMPLETE TIME PLOT OF EVENTS IN REVELATIONS CHAPTER 12 will help you with the sequence of events of that time. In MY UNDERSTANDING OF REVELATIONS 12, I detailed the events of this time so here I will just list them in chronological order with the pertinent scriptures.

The antichrist is first known from Daniels revelation (Dan 9:27) as mentioned above. At the very same time as the peace treaty is signed the two witnesses mentioned in Daniel 11v3 start prophesying for 1260 days clothed in sackcloth. Also, when the peace treaty is signed the antichrist allows Israel to build their new 3rd temple in Jerusalem, in which he wants to sit in and declare himself to be God, and so now focuses his attention on persecuting the church of Christ. This is the worst time for Christians. From the following extract from Matthew 24 we see that at this time Christians will be hated, tortured and killed, also many will be deceived by the false prophets so that many will be offended and be overcome:

> 9 "Then shall they deliver you up to be afflicted, and shall kill you: and ye shall be hated of all nations for my name's sake.
>
> 10 And then shall many be offended, and shall betray one another, and shall hate one another.
>
> 11 And many false prophets shall rise, and shall deceive many.
>
> 12 And because iniquity shall abound, the love of many shall wax cold."

Now we know what some of the citizens will be like in the last days from 2 Tim chap 3.
2 Tim 3:1-7

> "3 This know also, that in the last days perilous times shall come.
>
> 2 For men shall be lovers of their own selves, covetous, boasters, proud, blasphemers, disobedient to parents, unthankful, unholy,
>
> 3 Without natural affection, trucebreakers, false accusers, incontinent, fierce, despisers of those that are good,

4 Traitors, heady, high minded, lovers of pleasures more than lovers of God;

5 Having a form of godliness, but denying the power thereof: from such turn away.

6 For of this sort are they which creep into houses, and lead captive silly women laden with sins, led away with divers lusts,

7 Ever learning, and never able to come to the knowledge of the truth."

God's two witnesses

During this time the two witnesses prophesy for 1260 days (3,5YRS) and there is a great earthquake in which 7000 are killed. Rev 11:3-13

"3 And I will give power unto my two witnesses, and they shall prophesy a thousand two hundred and threescore days, clothed in sackcloth.

4 These are the two olive trees, and the two candlesticks standing before the God of the earth.

5 And if any man will hurt them, fire proceedeth out of their mouth, and devoureth their enemies: and if any man will hurt them, he must in this manner be killed.

6 These have power to shut heaven, that it rain not in the days of their prophecy: and have power over waters to turn them to blood, and to smite the earth with all plagues, as often as they will.

7 And when they shall have finished their testimony, the beast that ascendeth out of the bottomless pit shall make war against them, and shall overcome them, and kill them.

8 And their dead bodies shall lie in the street of the great city, which spiritually is called Sodom and Egypt, where also our Lord was crucified.

9 And they of the people and kindreds and tongues and nations shall see their dead bodies three days and an half, and shall not suffer their dead bodies to be put in graves.

10 And they that dwell upon the earth shall rejoice over them, and make merry, and shall send gifts one to another; because these two prophets tormented them that dwelt on the earth.

11 And after three days and an half the Spirit of life from God entered into them, and they stood upon their feet; and great fear fell upon them which saw them.

12 And they heard a great voice from heaven saying unto them, Come up hither. And they ascended up to heaven in a cloud; and their enemies beheld them.

13 And the same hour was there a great earthquake, and the tenth part of the city fell, and in the earthquake were slain of men seven thousand: and the remnant were affrighted, and gave glory to the God of heaven."

The mark of the beast

During this period the antichrist passes a law prohibiting anyone who does not have the name or mark of the beast from buying or selling, severely persecuting the Christians. We are told in Rev13 v16: "And he causeth all, both small and great, rich and poor, free and bond, to receive a mark in their right hand, or in their foreheads: and v17 "And that no man might buy or sell, save he that had the mark, or the name of the beast, or the number of his name."

There are also retributions from God for taking the mark. In Rev 14:9-11 we are told of them:

> "9 And the third angel followed them, saying with a loud voice, If any man worship the beast and his image, and receive his mark in his forehead, or in his hand,
>
> 10 The same shall drink of the wine of the wrath of God, which is poured out without mixture into the cup of his indignation; and he shall be tormented with fire and brimstone in the presence of the holy angels, and in the presence of the Lamb:
>
> 11 And the smoke of their torment ascendeth up for ever and ever: and they have no rest day nor night, who worship the beast and his image, and whosoever receiveth the mark of his name."

And in Rev 16:2 grievous sores: "2 And the first went, and poured out his vial upon the earth; and there fell a noisome and grievous sore upon the men which had the mark of the beast, and upon them which worshipped his image."

There are also rewards for those who persevere to the end. In Rev 15:2 we are told:

> "2 And I saw as it were a sea of glass mingled with fire: and them that had gotten the victory over the beast, and over his image, and over his mark, and over the number of his name, stand on the sea of glass, having the harps of God."

Commentary and Sunday law

I will now will discuss Rev 12v15 which I did not wish to deal with in the interpretation section of Rev chapter 12, but here in this commentary section. Rev 12v15 Reads "And the serpent cast out of his mouth water as a flood after the woman, that he might cause her to be carried away of the flood." Here a loose interpretation could be: a flood of something coming out of Satan's mouth threatening to wash the church or the Jews off their feet. I have been unable to further interpret Rev 12v15 from other scriptures alone but have been privileged to hear an angelic word on this subject. I have appended a section titled "ANNEXURE 3: THE ARK OF THE COVENANT" which explains how I received this information. As soon as the peace treaty is signed (see Dan 7:25 below) the antichrist will issue a decree called the Sunday Law, that God, must be worshiped on Sundays and not Fridays. This is a Balaam type trap for the Jews. Balaam was unable to curse the Israelites because they were blessed by God, so he advised the Moabites to cause the Israelites to sin and then God would curse them himself. So, if the Jews agreed they would be breaking the Law by not observing Ex 35:2 which says "Six days shall work be done, but on the seventh day there shall be to you an holy day, a sabbath of rest to the Lord: whosoever doeth work therein shall be put to death". So, the flood of water mentioned is the issue of a decree designed to either alienate the Jews from God or persecute them under the penalties of the antichrist law. At this time the Original Ten Commandment Tablets will be revealed (see ANNEXURE 3: THE ARK OF THE COVENANT) and it will also be announced that anyone who does not keep the fourth commandment to keep the Sabbath holy, will not go to heaven. This will be a dilemma for the observant Jews who will have choose between death if they disobey God or death if they disobey the antichrist. The Christians will not be alarmed at first because Sunday is their normal day of worship, but when they discover that the Church deliberately moved the Holy day from the Sabbath (Saturday) to Sunday and that Daniel warned us that the antichrist would attempt this, they will be challenged to keep the sabbath and be worn out by persecution: "And he shall speak great words against the most High, and shall wear out the saints of the most High, and think to change times and laws: and they shall be given into his hand until a time and times and the dividing of time" (Dan 7v25) or 3.5 years, or the full length of the completed peace treaty. Note that this verse shows that antichrist's authority will end after 3.5 years or at the middle of the peace treaty when events overtake the Sunday law. So, the flood that serpent cast out of his mouth is a decree to only worship God on Sundays and the rapture and the escape of the Jews at the end of the 1260 days nullifies it. The Sunday Law is already in effect in Germany and companies have already been fined for being open on Sunday but there is no world-wide edict yet.

And Verse 16: Here the reference to "the earth opened her mouth, and swallowed up the flood" occurs for the born-again Christians when they are delivered by the rapture, which takes place just before the Day of The Lord in the middle of the peace treaty. It is a picture of the dead in Christ rising first (1 Thess 4v16). Many of the Jews and unsaved Christians are also rescued at this time if they know and believe Jesus's warning and run for the hills when they see the abomination idol in the temple.

The image of the beast

Here because everything is interrelated and happens in quick succession, we will discuss some of it at the same time.

In Rev 13v12-14 the false prophet does wonders, bringing down fire from heaven, deceiving many and telling them to make an image to the beast. Rev 13:12-14 says:

> "12 And he exerciseth all the power of the first beast before him, and causeth the earth and them which dwell therein to worship the first beast, whose deadly wound was healed.
>
> 13 And he doeth great wonders, so that he maketh fire come down from heaven on the earth in the sight of men,
>
> 14 And deceiveth them that dwell on the earth by the means of those miracles which he had power to do in the sight of the beast; saying to them that dwell on the earth, that they should make an image to the beast, which had the wound by a sword, and did live."

In we read further in Dan 9v27 that the antichrist will terminate the peace treaty midway or after 1260 days or 3.5 years. Dan 9:27 "And he shall confirm the covenant with many for one week: and in the midst of the week he shall cause the sacrifice and the oblation to cease." After a 7 year peace covenant has been agreed the antichrist gains control of Jerusalem and then breaks the covenant in the middle of the 7 year period by stopping the daily sacrifice and oblation and erecting an idol called the "abomination of desolation" in the temple's holy of holies of the new 3rd Jewish Temple in Jerusalem. Now the false prophet had the power to give this idol life. In Rev 13v15 we read "And he had power to give life unto the image of the beast, that the image of the beast should both speak, and cause that as many as would not worship the image of the beast should be killed."

Start of the GREATEST TRIBULATION EVER

Now an immediate reaction takes place in heaven to the erection of the idol called the "abomination of desolation" in the Jew's temple's holy of holies.

Reading in Matt 24:15-22 given below, Jesus warns us (verse 16&21) to flee without delay to the mountains when we see or know of this idol as then there will be the worse tribulation ever. This tribulation is also known as the Lord's Day and the day of Wrath. It is the time when the lord rewards his saints and punishes those who destroyed his earth. See Rev 11:18: "And the nations were angry, and thy wrath is come, and the time of the dead, that they should be judged, and that thou shouldest give reward unto thy servants the prophets, and to the saints, and them that fear thy name, small and great; and shouldest destroy them which destroy the earth."

Also, Matt 24:

> "15 When ye therefore shall see the abomination of desolation, spoken of by Daniel the prophet, stand in the holy place, (whoso readeth, let him understand:)
>
> 16 Then let them which be in Judaea flee into the mountains:
>
> 17 Let him which is on the housetop not come down to take anything out of his house:
>
> 18 Neither let him which is in the field return back to take his clothes.

19 And woe unto them that are with child, and to them that give suck in those days!

20 But pray ye that your flight be not in the winter, neither on the sabbath day:

21 For then shall be great tribulation, such as was not since the beginning of the world to this time, no, nor ever shall be.

22 And except those days should be shortened, there should no flesh be saved: but for the elect's sake those days shall be shortened."

The elect in the KJV are the Jews. They are his chosen people (elected by Him) but will only ALL be saved at His 2nd second coming as described later.

CHAPTER 10

MY UNDERSTANDING OF THE CHRISTIAN RAPTURE

The rapture, also called the catching away of the Christians, is one of the most controversial prophesies in scripture. My minister and Professor Walter Veith, mentioned before, do not deny the rapture but only that it is not a secret one (a trumpet sounds) and that it only occurs at the time of Christ's single return. My minister has not published anything in this regard so only what I have mentioned is known. Professor Walter Veith has published a YouTube movie called the "SECRET RAPTURE DEBUNKED" giving all the scriptures he used to debunk it. I will first outline my understanding of the LAST DAYS EVENTS and their timing and afterwards check these against all the scriptures he has quoted to see if any of his do debunk a pre-tribulation rapture.

The most important scriptures for the rapture are 1 Thess 4:13-17 as given below:

> "13 But I would not have you to be ignorant, brethren, concerning them which are asleep, that ye sorrow not, even as others which have no hope.
>
> 14 For if we believe that Jesus died and rose again, even so them also which sleep in Jesus will God bring with him.

> 15 For this we say unto you by the word of the Lord, that we which are alive and remain unto the coming of the Lord shall not prevent them which are asleep.
>
> 16 For the Lord himself shall descend from heaven with a shout, with the voice of the archangel, and with the trump of God: and the dead in Christ shall rise first:
>
> 17 Then we which are alive and remain shall be caught up together with them in the clouds, to meet the Lord in the air: and so shall we ever be with the Lord."

Firstly, in the section titled CONTROVERSY SOLVED, I showed conclusively that although some believe in only 1 second coming, the 2 second comings is correct. Here it becomes very important not to get the 1 second coming the 2 second coming confused.

Now verse 14 indicates that Jesus brings the dead in Christ back with him in 2nd second coming, and then in verse 16 Paul tells us the dead in Christ shall rise first. This is not an error, both are correct. Paul also tells us in Phil 1v23: "For I am in a strait betwixt two, having a desire to depart, and to be with Christ; which is far better". He is telling us that those of us that die in Christ go immediately to be with the Lord but our bodies are buried! So, what the 1 Thess 4v13-17 scriptures are telling us is that when the Lord descends from heaven with the trump of God, he will bring with him the spiritual bodies of the dead saints whose earthly bodies will then rise from their graves to meet them in the air where they will become immaculate and put on immortality. Only then will we who are alive join them in the air in our new incorruptible bodies. This is confirmed by Paul in 1 Cor 15:51-53 below:

> "51 Behold, I shew you a mystery; We shall not all sleep, but we shall all be changed,
>
> 52 In a moment, in the twinkling of an eye, at the last trump: for the trumpet shall sound, and the dead shall be raised incorruptible, and we shall be changed.

> 53 For this corruptible must put on incorruption, and this mortal must put on immortality."

At the last trump we shall be changed but into what? Here is what the scriptures say:

So, from Luke 20:33-36 we see that Jesus said we will be like the angels.

Luke 20:33-36

> "33 Therefore in the resurrection whose wife of them is she? for seven had her to wife.
>
> 34 And Jesus answering said unto them, The children of this world marry, and are given in marriage:
>
> 35 But they which shall be accounted worthy to obtain that world, and the resurrection from the dead, neither marry, nor are given in marriage:
>
> 36 Neither can they die any more: for they are equal unto the angels; and are the children of God, being the children of the resurrection."

From 1 John 3v:2 we shall also be like the LORD.

> 2 "Beloved, now are we the sons of God, and it doth not yet appear what we shall be: but we know that, when he shall appear, we shall be like him; for we shall see him as he is."

And 1 Cor 2:16:

> "16 For who hath known the mind of the Lord, that he may instruct him? But we have the mind of Christ."

From 1 Cor 6:2-3 we see that we will be appointed as judges on the earth. This is not surprising as we will have the mind of Christ (see previous scripture) and no desire to sin. We will rule over the surviving nations and possibly Israel as well as angels (see scripture below) in the millennium.

1 Cor 6:2-3

"2 Do ye not know that the saints shall judge the world? and if the world shall be judged by you, are ye unworthy to judge the smallest matters?

3 Know ye not that we shall judge angels? how much more things that pertain to this life?"

Rev 5:10 further reigning

"10 And hast made us unto our God kings and priests: and we shall reign on the earth."

2 Tim 2:12 further reigning

12 "If we suffer, we shall also reign with him: if we deny him, he also will deny us:"

Now that we know all about the rapture, the big and very controversial problem is when will it happen? In Matt 24v36-44 (see below) Jesus tells us all about the time of the rapture.

"36 But of that day and hour knoweth no man, no, not the angels of heaven, but my Father only.

37 But as the days of Noe were, so shall also the coming of the Son of man be.

38 For as in the days that were before the flood they were eating and drinking, marrying and giving in marriage, until the day that Noe entered into the ark,

39 And knew not until the flood came, and took them all away; so shall also the coming of the Son of man be.

> 40 Then shall two be in the field; the one shall be taken, and the other left.
>
> 41 Two women shall be grinding at the mill; the one shall be taken, and the other left.
>
> 42 Watch therefore: for ye know not what hour your Lord doth come.
>
> 43 But know this, that if the goodman of the house had known in what watch the thief would come, he would have watched, and would not have suffered his house to be broken up.
>
> 44 Therefore be ye also ready: for in such an hour as ye think not the Son of man cometh."

I have received discouragement in the past from those who say that it is impossible to know the date or time of the rapture, quoting Matt 24:36 "But of that day and hour knoweth no man, no, not the angels of heaven, but my Father only" but this is not the whole truth. I will now show that alert Christians need not be taken by surprise. Firstly, let's look to see what the scriptures say about Christians escaping "THE DAY OF THE LORD" and his wrath. From the scriptures below we see that: if we judge ourselves we will not be judged; The wrath of God comes on the disobedient; and if we endure faithfully to the end he will keep us from the hour of testing; when the dead are judged we instead get rewards; Jesus has delivered us from the wrath to come; for God hath not appointed us to wrath but to salvation; being now justified by his blood we shall be saved from wrath through him; when the Pharisees and Sadducees came to be baptised, John said unto them "who has warned you to flee from the wrath to come", so the evidence above makes it very likely that the saints can escape the WRATH OF GOD to come.

1 Cor 11:31

> "31 For if we would judge ourselves, we should not be judged."

Col 3:6

"For which things' sake the wrath of God cometh on the children of disobedience:"

Rev 3:10

"Because thou hast kept the word of my patience, I also will keep thee from the hour of temptation, which shall come upon all the world, to try them that dwell upon the earth."

Rev 11:18

"And the nations were angry, and thy wrath is come, and the time of the dead, that they should be judged, and that thou shouldest give reward unto thy servants the prophets, and to the saints, and them that fear thy name, small and great; and shouldest destroy them which destroy the earth."

1 Thess 1v10

"10 And to wait for his Son from heaven, whom he raised from the dead, even Jesus, which delivered us from the wrath to come."

1 Thess 5v9

"For God hath not appointed us to wrath, but to obtain salvation by our Lord Jesus Christ,"

Rom 5v8-9

"8 But God commendeth his love toward us, in that, while we were yet sinners, Christ died for us."

9 Much more then, being now justified by his blood, we shall be saved from wrath through him.

Matt 3v7

> "7 But when he saw many of the Pharisees and Sadducees come to his baptism, he said unto them, O generation of vipers, who hath warned you to flee from the wrath to come?"

Luke 21:34-36

> "34 And take heed to yourselves, lest at any time your hearts be overcharged with surfeiting, and drunkenness, and cares of this life, and so that day come upon you unawares."
>
> 35 For as a snare shall it come on all them that dwell on the face of the whole earth.
>
> 36 Watch ye therefore, and pray always, that ye may be accounted worthy to escape all these things that shall come to pass, and to stand before the Son of man."

In the last scripture above, Luke 21v34-36: "That ye may be accounted worthy to escape" we see that escape is conditional. I see this as not as affecting the time of the rapture but who will be raptured. It is not possible for diligent saints to remain awake for years without sleeping. So here we are talking about being spiritually awake. We can confirm this from Luke 17v34: "I tell you, in that night there shall be two men in one bed; the one shall be taken, and the other shall be left." So, one was taken while he was asleep. We can see who will be raptured by the greeting you will get when you get there. In Matt 25v21: "His lord said unto him, Well done, thou good and faithful servant: thou hast been faithful over a few things, I will make thee ruler over many things: enter thou into the joy of thy lord." So, we see that the good and faithful servants (saints) get in. We are now sure that the rapture happens before the day of the Lord's wrath but no idea when.

In Luke 21v20-28 (see below) Jesus discusses this time.

"20 And when ye shall see Jerusalem compassed with armies, then know that the desolation thereof is nigh.

21 Then let them which are in Judaea flee to the mountains; and let them which are in the midst of it depart out; and let not them that are in the countries enter thereinto.

22 For these be the days of vengeance, that all things which are written may be fulfilled.

23 But woe unto them that are with child, and to them that give suck, in those days! for there shall be great distress in the land, and wrath upon this people.

24 And they shall fall by the edge of the sword, and shall be led away captive into all nations: and Jerusalem shall be trodden down of the Gentiles, until the times of the Gentiles be fulfilled.

25 And there shall be signs in the sun, and in the moon, and in the stars; and upon the earth distress of nations, with perplexity; the sea and the waves roaring;

26 Men's hearts failing them for fear, and for looking after those things which are coming on the earth: for the powers of heaven shall be shaken.

27 And then shall they see the Son of man coming in a cloud with power and great glory.

28 And when these things begin to come to pass, then look up, and lift up your heads; for your redemption draweth nigh."

A summary of the above could read:
When you see Jerusalem surrounded by armies know that the days of vengeance and wrath have come. There will be a war over Jerusalem, many will be killed and many taken captive. Jerusalem

will then be captured and ruled by the Gentiles. At this time there will be signs in the sun, the moon and the stars for the powers of heaven will be shaken, and then they will see Jesus come in the clouds with power and great glory. The trumpet blast is not mentioned here. When you see these things begin to happen, look up for your salvation is at hand.

There is an amazing amount of information contained in these verses, so let us unpack it.

Firstly, we see we are at the 1 second coming because the saints are still on earth waiting for redemption. In verse 28 speaking to the saints Jesus says "And when these things begin to come to pass, then look up, and lift up your heads; for your redemption draweth nigh." The "with power and great glory" (verse 27) part reflects His huge power and authority when he brings back the spirits of all the dead saints with him, raises their dead bodies and then unites them in new incorruptible bodies. This power then raises the living saints into the air to join him, also with new incorruptible bodies.

Secondly the sound of the trump (1 Cor 15:51 above) is not mentioned, concealing the timing of the rapture from us. It has not yet happened when these events begin to happen because we are still there and told to look up as our salvation is near.

Thirdly when the Armageddon War armies assemble to attack Jerusalem there will be great concern in the city, and at this time the saints will be hoping and praying for their salvation.

Fourthly these events show that the Armageddon War starts prior to Jerusalem being taken. In the 70 AD Roman siege of Jerusalem the priests continued their duties even after the temple was taken and had to be killed to stop the sacrifices. This is likely to be the same again, so the antichrist will only be able to stop them sacrificing after the city and temple were taken.

Fifthly, since we know there will be no warning of the rapture, the verse 25 signs in the sky and earth will not have taken place yet. Also, the people will be taken by surprise. Matt 24v37 "But as the days of Noe were, so shall also the coming of the Son of man be." And verse 39 "And knew not until the flood came, and took them all away; so shall also the coming of the Son of man be." Hence the saints were raptured before anyone noticed that bad things were about to happen.

So, we can say the rapture happens as soon as the first signs of the attack are noticed.

Sixthly, the antichrist will only be able to erect his idol in the Jewish temple after he has subdued Jerusalem and stopped the daily sacrifice. The erection of this idol causes the immediate start of the greatest tribulation ever, also called "THE DAY OF THE LORD'S WRATH" (see Matt 24v15 above).

Timing of the rapture event resolved

Since we know that the rapture comes without warning as in the days of Noah, (Mat 24v39 "And knew not until the flood came, and took them all away; so shall also the coming of the Son of man be.", and because we know the saints are not judged twice, it must precede the "day of the lord's wrath".

So, in order to determine the timing of the rapture event I have mapped the sequence of the events below:

1. Jerusalem is surrounded by the Antichrist armies. (Luke 21v20-22 see above). Here we are warned of Jerusalem's imminent destruction and that these are the days of God's vengeance. The inhabitants of Jerusalem and neighbouring Judea are warned to flee.
2. The stopping of the daily sacrifice.
3. The erection of the "abomination that makes desolate" idol. Here his disciples are again warned to flee Jerusalem.

All three of the above events can be construed as warnings so I have concluded the rapture must precede them all. This however creates a quandary. In Mathew 24v14&15 Jesus, speaking to his disciples and subsequent readers, tells them to flee when they see the idol in the temple. His disciples will not have been there to see the idol if the rapture has already taken place. I offer this explanation for this quandary. The saints have been raptured but Jesus was not only speaking to his disciples but also to the Jews and nominal Christians who are left behind.

THE CAPTURE OF JERUSALEM AND THE ARMAGEDDON WAR

I have just found above that this war starts just after the rapture and before the daily sacrifice is stopped, which ends the peace treaty. The following scriptures from Dan 11 are of the antichrist and although not clear it seems to show that he enters the holy land deceitfully.

Dan 11:

> "21 And in his estate shall stand up a vile person, to whom they shall not give the honour of the kingdom: but he shall come in peaceably, and obtain the kingdom by flatteries.
>
> 22 And with the arms of a flood shall they be overflown from before him, and shall be broken; yea, also the prince of the covenant.
>
> 23 And after the league made with him he shall work deceitfully: for he shall come up, and shall become strong with a small people.
>
> 24 He shall enter peaceably even upon the fattest places of the province"

The following scriptures show the antichrist is against the holy covenant and will come with an army and take away the daily sacrifice, and then erect the abomination that makes desolate, idol. He will do wickedly and destroy many by the sword, by flame, by captivity, and by spoil, for many days.

Dan 11 continues:

> "30 For the ships of Chittim shall come against him: therefore he shall be grieved, and return, and have indignation against the holy covenant: so shall he do; he shall even return, and have intelligence with them that forsake the holy covenant.

> 31 And arms shall stand on his part, and they shall pollute the sanctuary of strength, and shall take away the daily sacrifice, and they shall place the abomination that maketh desolate.
>
> 32 And such as do wickedly against the covenant shall he corrupt by flatteries: but the people that do know their God shall be strong, and do exploits.
>
> 33 And they that understand among the people shall instruct many: yet they shall fall by the sword, and by flame, by captivity, and by spoil, many days.

He will then magnify himself to be God:

> "36 And the king shall do according to his will; and he shall exalt himself, and magnify himself above every god, and shall speak marvellous things against the God of gods, and shall prosper till the indignation be accomplished: for that that is determined shall be done."

Now when he enters the holy land, he will overthrow many countries but the following will escape, Edom, Moab, and the chief of the children of Ammon. This is where the Woman (Israel) will be sheltered from the tribulation. And after that, the antichrist will be destroyed.

> "41 He shall enter also into the glorious land, and many countries shall be overthrown: but these shall escape out of his hand, even Edom, and Moab, and the chief of the children of Ammon.
>
> 45 And he shall plant the tabernacles of his palace between the seas in the glorious holy mountain; yet he shall come to his end, and none shall help him."

In Revelation 16 we are told that it is the evil spirits that control the kings and gather them for the battle of Armageddon.

Rev 16

> "14 For they are the spirits of devils, working miracles, which go forth unto the kings of the earth and of the whole world, to gather them to the battle of that great day of God Almighty.
>
> 16 And he gathered them together into a place called in the Hebrew tongue Armageddon."

Some of the scriptures above are a little clouded by history so the best understanding of the war comes from the revelation John received in Revelations chapter 19 given below.

A paraphrase could read:

Jesus comes riding on a white horse to judge and make war with Satan and his armies. His eyes flame like fire, he is wearing many crowns on his head and his clothing is covered in blood. The armies of heaven follow him, also on white horses and clothed in white linen. His word is like a sharp sword in his mouth to judge and make war and he destroys the evil fruit of the nations in his anger like grapes in a wine press. John sees the beast, the kings of the earth and their armies gathered together to make war against Jesus and his army. The beast is captured and the false prophet that made the miracles to deceived those that had received the mark of the beast and who worshipped his image. These two were both cast alive into a lake of fire. And the remnants were slain with sword that proceeded out of Jesus's mouth. An angel in heaven then calls all the birds to come to the great feast called "the supper of the great God". And they will eat the flesh of kings, captains, mighty men and horses.

Rev 19:11-21

> "11 And I saw heaven opened, and behold a white horse; and he that sat upon him was called Faithful and True, and in righteousness he doth judge and make war.
>
> 12 His eyes were as a flame of fire, and on his head were many crowns; and he had a name written, that no man knew, but he himself. And on his cloak he

had written "KING OF KINGS AND LORD OF LORDS".

13 And he was clothed with a vesture dipped in blood: and his name is called The Word of God.

14 And the armies which were in heaven followed him upon white horses, clothed in fine linen, white and clean.

15 And out of his mouth goeth a sharp sword, that with it he should smite the nations: and he shall rule them with a rod of iron: and he treadeth the winepress of the fierceness and wrath of Almighty God.

16 And he hath on his vesture and on his thigh a name written, KING OF KINGS, AND LORD OF LORDS.

17 And I saw an angel standing in the sun; and he cried with a loud voice, saying to all the fowls that fly in the midst of heaven, Come and gather yourselves together unto the supper of the great God;

18 That ye may eat the flesh of kings, and the flesh of captains, and the flesh of mighty men, and the flesh of horses, and of them that sit on them, and the flesh of all men, both free and bond, both small and great.

19 And I saw the beast, and the kings of the earth, and their armies, gathered together to make war against him that sat on the horse, and against his army.

20 And the beast was taken, and with him the false prophet that wrought miracles before him, with which he deceived them that had received the mark of the beast, and them that worshipped his image. These both were cast alive into a lake of fire burning with brimstone.

> 21 And the remnant were slain with the sword of him that sat upon the horse, which sword proceeded out of his mouth: and all the fowls were filled with their flesh."

Then lastly here is an extract from Joel 3 that gives more information on this battle.

> "2 I will also gather all nations, and will bring them down into the valley of Jehoshaphat, and will plead with them there for my people and for my heritage Israel, whom they have scattered among the nations, and parted my land.
>
> 9 Proclaim ye this among the Gentiles; Prepare war, wake up the mighty men, let all the men of war draw near; let them come up:
>
> 10 Beat your plowshares into swords, and your pruninghooks into spears: let the weak say, I am strong.
>
> 11 Assemble yourselves, and come, all ye heathen, and gather yourselves together round about: thither cause thy mighty ones to come down, O Lord.
>
> 12 Let the heathen be wakened, and come up to the valley of Jehoshaphat: for there will I sit to judge all the heathen round about.
>
> 13 Put ye in the sickle, for the harvest is ripe: come, get you down; for the press is full, the fats overflow; for their wickedness is great.
>
> 14 Multitudes, multitudes in the valley of decision: for the day of the Lord is near in the valley of decision.
>
> 15 The sun and the moon shall be darkened, and the stars shall withdraw their shining.

16 The Lord also shall roar out of Zion, and utter his voice from Jerusalem; and the heavens and the earth shall shake: but the Lord will be the hope of his people, and the strength of the children of Israel.

17 So shall ye know that I am the Lord your God dwelling in Zion, my holy mountain: then shall Jerusalem be holy, and there shall no strangers pass through her any more.

18 And it shall come to pass in that day, that the mountains shall drop down new wine, and the hills shall flow with milk, and all the rivers of Judah shall flow with waters, and a fountain shall come forth of the house of the Lord, and shall water the valley of Shittim."

A description of the battle for Jerusalem and the consequences thereof

Zechariah 14:

"**12** And this shall be the plague wherewith the Lord will smite all the people that have fought against Jerusalem; Their flesh shall consume away while they stand upon their feet, and their eyes shall consume away in their holes, and their tongue shall consume away in their mouth.

13 And it shall come to pass in that day, that a great tumult from the Lord shall be among them; and they shall lay hold everyone on the hand of his neighbour, and his hand shall rise up against the hand of his neighbour.

14 And Judah also shall fight at Jerusalem; and the wealth of all the heathen round about shall be gathered together, gold, and silver, and apparel, in great abundance.

15 And so shall be the plague of the horse, of the mule, of the camel, and of the ass, and of all the beasts that shall be in these tents, as this plague."

CHAPTER 11

THE 2ND 3.5 YEARS OF THE ANTICHRIST'S RULE

The 2nd 3.5 years of the Antichrist's rule starts with the GREATEST TRIBULATION EVER judgements

In addition to all the misery created by the antichrist in the first 3.5 years of his reign he now erects his idol in the holy of holies in the new Jewish temple and the GREATEST TRIBULATION EVER BEGINS. In Matt 24 Jesus warns us of the greatest tribulation that will ever be. Matt 24:15: says "When ye therefore shall see the abomination of desolation, spoken of by Daniel the prophet, stand in the holy place, ….. and Matt 24:21 "For then shall be great tribulation, such as was not since the beginning of the world to this time, no, nor ever shall be."

Here is a summary of these judgements:

Rev 6:

"12 And I beheld when he had opened the sixth seal, and, lo, there was a great earthquake; and the sun became black as sackcloth of hair, and the moon became as blood;

> 13 And the stars of heaven fell unto the earth, even as a fig tree casts her untimely figs, when she is shaken of a mighty wind.
>
> 14 And the heaven departed as a scroll when it is rolled together; and every mountain and island were moved out of their places."

More worldly calamities.
Rev 8:

> "5 And the angel took the censer, and filled it with fire of the altar, and cast it into the earth: and there were voices, and thunderings, and lightnings, and an earthquake.
>
> 6 And the seven angels which had the seven trumpets prepared themselves to sound.
>
> 7 The first angel sounded, and there followed hail and fire mingled with blood, and they were cast upon the earth: and the third part of trees was burnt up, and all green grass was burnt up.
>
> 8 And the second angel sounded, and as it were a great mountain burning with fire was cast into the sea: and the third part of the sea became blood;
>
> 9 And the third part of the creatures which were in the sea, and had life, died; and the third part of the ships were destroyed.
>
> 10 And the third angel sounded, and there fell a great star from heaven, burning as it were a lamp, and it fell upon the third part of the rivers, and upon the fountains of waters;
>
> 11 And the name of the star is called Wormwood: and the third part of the waters became wormwood;

and many men died of the waters, because they were made bitter.

12 And the fourth angel sounded, and the third part of the sun was smitten, and the third part of the moon, and the third part of the stars; so as the third part of them was darkened, and the day shone not for a third part of it, and the night likewise."

In Revelations chapter 9 a plague of demonic locusts molests the people for 5 months.

"3 And there came out of the smoke locusts upon the earth: and unto them was given power, as the scorpions of the earth have power.

4 And it was commanded them that they should not hurt the grass of the earth, neither any green thing, neither any tree; but only those men which have not the seal of God in their foreheads.

5 And to them it was given that they should not kill them, but that they should be tormented five months: and their torment was as the torment of a scorpion, when he striketh a man.

6 And in those days shall men seek death, and shall not find it; and shall desire to die, and death shall flee from them.

7 And the shapes of the locusts were like unto horses prepared unto battle; and on their heads were as it were crowns like gold, and their faces were as the faces of men.

8 And they had hair as the hair of women, and their teeth were as the teeth of lions.

9 And they had breastplates, as it were breastplates of iron; and the sound of their wings was as the sound of chariots of many horses running to battle.

10 And they had tails like unto scorpions, and there were stings in their tails: and their power was to hurt men five months.

11 And they had a king over them, which is the angel of the bottomless pit, whose name in the Hebrew tongue is Abaddon, but in the Greek tongue hath his name Apollyon."

After this the plague of 200 000 000 demonic horsemen is released to cross the dried-up Euphrates River and kill 1/3 of all people.

Rev 9:

"14 Saying to the sixth angel which had the trumpet, Loose the four angels which are bound in the great river Euphrates.

15 And the four angels were loosed, which were prepared for an hour, and a day, and a month, and a year, for to slay the third part of men.

16 And the number of the army of the horsemen were two hundred thousand thousand: and I heard the number of them.

17 And thus I saw the horses in the vision, and them that sat on them, having breastplates of fire, and of jacinth, and brimstone: and the heads of the horses were as the heads of lions; and out of their mouths issued fire and smoke and brimstone.

18 By these three was the third part of men killed, by the fire, and by the smoke, and by the brimstone, which issued out of their mouths.

> 19 For their power is in their mouth, and in their tails: for their tails were like unto serpents, and had heads, and with them they do hurt."

Rev 14:19-20 describes the gathering of all God's enemies into his winepress.

> "19 And the angel thrust in his sickle into the earth, and gathered the vine of the earth, and cast it into the great winepress of the wrath of God.
>
> 20 And the winepress was trodden without the city, and blood came out of the winepress, even unto the horse bridles, by the space of a thousand and six hundred furlongs" (or 200 miles).

And from Revelation 16 the vial judgements:

Verse 2: "a noisome and grievous sore upon the men which had the mark of the beast, and upon them which worshipped his image."
Verse 3: "And the second angel poured out his vial upon the sea; and it became as the blood of a dead man: and every living soul died in the sea."
Verse 4: "the rivers and fountains of waters became blood."
Verse 6: "they have shed the blood of saints and prophets, and thou hast given them blood to drink"
Verse 9: "And men were scorched with great heat"
Verse 10: "the fifth angel poured out his vial upon the seat of the beast; and his kingdom was full of darkness; and they gnawed their tongues for pain"
Verse 18: "and there was a great earthquake, such as was not since men were upon the earth, so mighty an earthquake, and so great."
Verse 19: "And the great city was divided into three parts, and the cities of the nations fell"
Verse 20: "And every island fled away, and the mountains were not found."

Verse 21: "And there fell upon men a great hail out of heaven, every stone about the weight of a talent (about 60kg): and men blasphemed God because of the plague of the hail; for the plague thereof was exceeding great."

Rev 18:6-8 the judgement of the great whore:

"6 Reward her even as she rewarded you, and double unto her double according to her works: in the cup which she hath filled fill to her double.

7 How much she hath glorified herself, and lived deliciously, so much torment and sorrow give her: for she saith in her heart, I sit a queen, and am no widow, and shall see no sorrow.

8 Therefore shall her plagues come in one day, death, and mourning, and famine; and she shall be utterly burned with fire: for strong is the Lord God who judgeth her.

20 Rejoice over her, thou heaven, and ye holy apostles and prophets; for God hath avenged you on her.

21 And a mighty angel took up a stone like a great millstone, and cast it into the sea, saying, Thus with violence shall that great city Babylon be thrown down, and shall be found no more at all."

CHAPTER 12

THE 2ND SECOND COMING OF THE LORD AT THE END OF THE GREATEST TRIBULATION EVER

From Zechariah 14 we read of the Lord's 2nd second coming when he stands on the mount of olives after he defeats the antichrist.

Zechariah 14:

> "1 Behold, the day of the Lord cometh, and thy spoil shall be divided in the midst of thee.
>
> 2 For I will gather all nations against Jerusalem to battle; and the city shall be taken, and the houses rifled, and the women ravished; and half of the city shall go forth into captivity, and the residue of the people shall not be cut off from the city.
>
> 3 Then shall the Lord go forth, and fight against those nations, as when he fought in the day of battle.
>
> 4 And his feet shall stand in that day upon the mount of Olives, which is before Jerusalem on the east, and

the mount of Olives shall cleave in the midst thereof toward the east and toward the west, and there shall be a very great valley; and half of the mountain shall remove toward the north, and half of it toward the south.

5 And ye shall flee to the valley of the mountains; for the valley of the mountains shall reach unto Azal: yea, ye shall flee, like as ye fled from before the earthquake in the days of Uzziah king of Judah: and the Lord my God shall come, and all the saints with thee.

6 And it shall come to pass in that day, that the light shall not be clear, nor dark:

7 But it shall be one day which shall be known to the Lord, not day, nor night: but it shall come to pass, that at evening time it shall be light.

8 And it shall be in that day, that living waters shall go out from Jerusalem; half of them toward the former sea, and half of them toward the hinder sea: in summer and in winter shall it be.

9 And the Lord shall be king over all the earth: in that day shall there be one Lord, and his name one.

10 All the land shall be turned as a plain from Geba to Rimmon south of Jerusalem: and it shall be lifted up, and inhabited in her place, from Benjamin's gate unto the place of the first gate, unto the corner gate, and from the tower of Hananeel unto the king's winepresses.

11 And men shall dwell in it, and there shall be no more utter destruction; but Jerusalem shall be safely inhabited."

The end of the Antichrist's and Satan's reign

The beast, false prophet and Satan are judged.
Rev 19:

> "20 And the beast was taken, and with him the false prophet that wrought miracles before him, with which he deceived them that had received the mark of the beast, and them that worshipped his image. These both were cast alive into a lake of fire burning with brimstone."

Rev 20

> "1 And I saw an angel come down from heaven, having the key of the bottomless pit and a great chain in his hand.
>
> 2 And he laid hold on the dragon, that old serpent, which is the Devil, and Satan, and bound him a thousand years,
>
> 3 And cast him into the bottomless pit, and shut him up, and set a seal upon him, that he should deceive the nations no more, till the thousand years should be fulfilled: and after that he must be loosed a little season."

It is time for the saints to be rewarded

This needs careful explanation. The saints, the living and dead will be raptured, given immortal bodies and then forever be with the Lord. They will have already been washed in the blood of Jesus and judged guiltless while alive. This is the called first resurrection. There will be a second resurrection for all those still dead, for them to be present at the GREAT WHITE THRONE JUDGEMENT after the millennium. The saints will be exempt from this judgement, called the second death, as they have already been judged.

Rev 20

> "4 And I saw thrones, and they sat upon them, and judgment was given unto them: and I saw the souls of them that were beheaded for the witness of Jesus, and for the word of God, and which had not worshipped the beast, neither his image, neither had received his mark upon their foreheads, or in their hands; and they lived and reigned with Christ a thousand years.
>
> 5 But the rest of the dead lived not again until the thousand years were finished. This is the first resurrection.
>
> 6 Blessed and holy is he that hath part in the first resurrection: on such the second death hath no power, but they shall be priests of God and of Christ, and shall reign with him a thousand years."

What happens to Israel?

All Israel will be raised from the dead, if dead, and all of them pardoned at the beginning of the millennium. They will then be resurrected, if required, at the end of the millennium and only finally judged at the white throne judgement. They have been given a get out of jail free card for the start of the millennium. This by the grace of God alone, presumably because of all the enmity they suffered by being seen as the closeted chosen children of God. They will then have no excuses when they are judged at the white throne judgement.

> 7 "Alas! for that day is great, so that none is like it: it is even the time of Jacob's trouble; but he shall be saved out of it.
>
> 8 For it shall come to pass in that day, saith the Lord of hosts, that I will break his yoke from off thy neck, and will burst thy bonds, and strangers shall no more serve themselves of him:" Jer 30:7-8

> 25 For I would not, brethren, that ye should be ignorant of this mystery, lest ye should be wise in your own conceits; that blindness in part is happened to Israel, until the fulness of the Gentiles be come in.
>
> 26 And so all Israel shall be saved: as it is written, There shall come out of Sion the Deliverer, and shall turn away ungodliness from Jacob:
>
> 27 For this is my covenant unto them, when I shall take away their sins. Rom 11:25-27

The marriage supper of the Lamb

This takes place in heaven immediately after the first resurrection and is a 3.5 year celebration of the saint's victory over Satan and their marriage to the Lamb. There is now great rejoicing in heaven as the righteous are all there, celebrating after being raptured, but on earth there is a huge contrast as God is pouring out his wrath on the wicked who rejected Him, for the great day of the Lord has come.
Rev 19:

> "9 marriage of the Lamb is come, and his wife hath made herself ready.
>
> 8 And to her was granted that she should be arrayed in fine linen, clean and white: for the fine linen is the righteousness of saints.
>
> 9 And he saith unto me, Write, Blessed are they which are called unto the marriage supper of the Lamb."

MY FINAL CONCLUSION

I have above presented my understanding of the last days events and their timing with all the scriptures pertinent to this period and concluded that there will be a pre-tribulation rapture and two 2nd comings.

For those who wish to see how Walter came to his conclusion, I will now review all the scriptures Professor Walter Veith published in his YouTube movie called the "SECRET RAPTURE DEBUNKED" and test them against those given above to see if any of them do debunk the PRE-TRIBULATION RAPTURE and the TWO SECOND COMINGS OF CHRIST. (Interpretation 2).

CHAPTER 13

A REVIEW OF THE SCRIPTURE'S PROFESSOR WALTER VEITH USED TO MAKE HIS CLAIM TO HAVE DEBUNKED THE "SECRET RAPTURE"

Professor Walter Veith's scriptures supporting interpretation 1, only 1 second coming, from his YouTube video "secret rapture debunked" are given below followed by my comments.

Scripture 1:

> Ex 5:4 And the king of Egypt said unto them, Wherefore do ye, Moses and Aaron, let the people from their works? get you unto your burdens. KJV

My comment: This scripture has no relevance to the discussion above.

Scripture 2:

> Rev 15:1 And I saw another sign in heaven, great and marvellous, seven angels having the seven last plagues; for in them is filled up the wrath of God. KJV

My comment: This scripture also has no relevance to the discussion above.

Scripture 3:

> Titus 2:13 Looking for that blessed hope, and the glorious appearing of the great God and our Saviour Jesus Christ; KJV

Here he says we are not without hope but are looking forward to Jesus.
My comment: No relevance.

Scripture 4:
He then lists the 4 comings of Christ, as a babe, to the Ancient of Days (Dan 7v13), second coming, and to restore the earth and set up the kingdom. My comment: This last is possibly the new heaven and new earth. No details given so not relevant.

Scripture 5:

> Isa 7:14 Therefore the Lord himself shall give you a sign; Behold, a virgin shall conceive, and bear a son, and shall call his name Immanuel. KJV

My comment: His comment is the Jews ignored this one, his first coming. Not relevant.

Scripture 6:

> Matt 1:23 Behold, a virgin shall be with child, and shall bring forth a son, and they shall call his name

Emmanuel, which being interpreted is, God with us. KJV

My comment: same.

Scripture 7:

> Isa 53:5 But he was wounded for our transgressions, he was bruised for our iniquities: the chastisement of our peace was upon him; and with his stripes we are healed. KJV

His comment is the Jews ignored this one too, they were waiting for someone else.
My comment: Not relevant.

Scripture 8:

> John 14:2-3 In my Father's house are many mansions: if it were not so, I would have told you. I go to prepare a place for you.
>
> 3 And if I go and prepare a place for you, I will come again, and receive you unto myself; that where I am, there ye may be also. KJV

My comment: His comment is that He is coming again because he wants to receive us to himself. Not relevant.

Scripture 9:

> Rev 1:7 Behold, he cometh with clouds; and every eye shall see him, and they also which pierced him: and all kindreds of the earth shall wail because of him. Even so, Amen. KJV

My comment: His comment is that His second coming will be universally visible so nobody will NOT know that he has come, so there cannot be a secret rapture. He is entirely correct but only for the

2nd second coming and not the 1st second coming. See my comment on his Scripture 12.

Scripture 10:

> Matt 24:27 For as the lightning cometh out of the east, and shineth even unto the west; so shall also the coming of the Son of man be. KJV

My comment: same.

Scripture 11:

> Ps 104:3 Who layeth the beams of his chambers in the waters: who maketh the clouds his chariot: who walketh upon the wings of the wind: KJV

Comment: He says the clouds mentioned can also be chariots as in the Psalm above.
My comment: Not relevant.

Scripture 12:

> Ps 68:3 The chariots of God are twenty thousand, even thousands of angels: the Lord is among them, as in Sinai, in the holy place. KJV

My comment: He says the clouds are the chariots of God bringing thousands and thousands of angels with Him when He comes. Not relevant.

Scripture 13:

> Matt 24:30 And then shall appear the sign of the Son of man in heaven: and then shall all the tribes of the earth mourn, and they shall see the Son of man coming in the clouds of heaven with power and great glory. KJV

My comment: He says this confirms that Jesus is coming with His angels. However, in 1 Thess 4:13-17 where the rapture of the dead and living saints is foretold, it does mention the voice of the archangel and the trump of God, but makes no mention of any angels. It does not portray the glorious and triumphant return of Christ but a rather quick collection of all the saints. So, this not the same return he is talking about but a very differ one, the first second coming.

Scripture 14:

> 2 Thess 1:7 And to you who are troubled rest with us, when the Lord Jesus shall be revealed from heaven with his mighty angels, KJV

My comment: He tries to confirm again that Jesus is coming with His angels but this says "revealed" and not coming and is not specific to how, where or on which occasion.

Scripture 15:

> Matt 25:31 When the Son of man shall come in his glory, and all the holy angels with him, then shall he sit upon the throne of his glory: KJV

My comment: He says this confirms that Jesus is coming with ALL His angels. Again, this is His 2nd second coming and not the first.

Scripture 16:

> Luke 9:26 For whosoever shall be ashamed of me and of my words, of him shall the Son of man be ashamed, when he shall come in his own glory, and in his Father's, and of the holy angels. KJV

My comment: not relevant.

Scripture 17:

> Rev 5:11 And I beheld, and I heard the voice of many angels round about the throne and the beasts and the elders: and the number of them was ten thousand times ten thousand, and thousands of thousands; KJV

My comment: not relevant.

Scripture 18:

> Acts 1:11 Which also said, Ye men of Galilee, why stand ye gazing up into heaven? this same Jesus, which is taken up from you into heaven, shall so come in like manner as ye have seen him go into heaven. KJV

My comment: does not add anything.

Scripture 19:

> 1 Thess 4:16 For the Lord himself shall descend from heaven with a shout, with the voice of the archangel, and with the trump of God: and the dead in Christ shall rise first: KJV

My comment: Agreed but happens at the 1st second coming.

Scripture 20:

> Matt 24:31 And he shall send his angels with a great sound of a trumpet, and they shall gather together his elect from the four winds, from one end of heaven to the other. KJV

My comment: Agreed but happens at the 2nd second coming when after the tribulation he gathers all resurrected Israel, his elect, to Him in their new mortal bodies.

Scripture 21:

> 1 Thess 4:16-17 For the Lord himself shall descend from heaven with a shout, with the voice of the archangel, and with the trump of God: and the dead in Christ shall rise first:
>
> 17 Then we which are alive and remain shall be caught up together with them in the clouds, to meet the Lord in the air: and so shall we ever be with the Lord. KJV

> My comment: Agreed but again happens at the 1st second coming.

Scripture 22:

> Matt 24:26-27 Wherefore if they shall say unto you, Behold, he is in the desert; go not forth: behold, he is in the secret chambers; believe it not. 27 For as the lightning cometh out of the east, and shineth even unto the west; so shall also the coming of the Son of man be. KJV

> My comment: again not secret but not pertinent.

Scripture 23:

> 1 Thess 4:16 For the Lord himself shall descend from heaven with a shout, with the voice of the archangel, and with the trump of God: and the dead in Christ shall rise first: KJV

> My comment: Repeat. Same comment.

Scripture 24:

> Rev 20:5-6 But the rest of the dead lived not again until the thousand years were finished. This is the first resurrection. 6 Blessed and holy is he that hath

> part in the first resurrection: on such the second death hath no power, but they shall be priests of God and of Christ, and shall reign with him a thousand years. KJV

My comment: There is only one first resurrection which happens at the 1st second coming and is only for believers. The second resurrection and second death are for sinners only.

Scripture 25:

> Rev 20:5-6 But the rest of the dead lived not again until the thousand years were finished. This is the first resurrection. 6 Blessed and holy is he that hath part in the first resurrection: on such the second death hath no power, but they shall be priests of God and of Christ, and shall reign with him a thousand years. KJV

My comment: see previous.

Scripture 26:

> 1 Cor 15:52-53 In a moment, in the twinkling of an eye, at the last trump: for the trumpet shall sound, and the dead shall be raised incorruptible, and we shall be changed. 53 For this corruptible must put on incorruption, and this mortal must put on immortality. KJV

My comment: He says that everything will then be changed and nothing will die anymore. Not relevant.

Scripture 27:

> Phil 3:20-21 For our conversation is in heaven; from whence also we look for the Saviour, the Lord Jesus Christ: 21 Who shall change our vile body, that it may be fashioned like unto his glorious body, according to

the working whereby he is able even to subdue all things unto himself. KJV

My comment: He says we get a body like Jesus's. Not relevant.

Scripture 28:

Matt 13:49-50 So shall it be at the end of the world: the angels shall come forth, and sever the wicked from among the just, 50 And shall cast them into the furnace of fire: there shall be wailing and gnashing of teeth. KJV

My comment: Not pertinent.

Scripture 29:

Rev 6:15-17 And the kings of the earth, and the great men, and the rich men, and the chief captains, and the mighty men, and every bondman, and every free man, hid themselves in the dens and in the rocks of the mountains; 16 And said to the mountains and rocks, Fall on us, and hide us from the face of him that sitteth on the throne, and from the wrath of the Lamb: 17 For the great day of his wrath is come; and who shall be able to stand? KJV

My comment: Not pertinent.

Scripture 30:

Matt 24:30 And then shall appear the sign of the Son of man in heaven: and then shall all the tribes of the earth mourn, and they shall see the Son of man coming in the clouds of heaven with power and great glory. KJV

My comment: 2nd second coming when seen by all.

Scripture 31:

> Jude 14-15 And Enoch also, the seventh from Adam, prophesied of these, saying, Behold, the Lord cometh with ten thousands of his saints, 15 To execute judgment upon all, and to convince all that are ungodly among them of all their ungodly deeds which they have ungodly committed, and of all their hard speeches which ungodly sinners have spoken against him. KJV

My comment: again 2nd second coming when seen by all.

Scripture 32:

> Zeph 1:14-15 The great day of the Lord is near, it is near, and hasteth greatly, even the voice of the day of the Lord: the mighty man shall cry there bitterly. 15 That day is a day of wrath, a day of trouble and distress, a day of wasteness and desolation, a day of darkness and gloominess, a day of clouds and thick darkness, KJV

My comment: the time of the greatest tribulation ever.

Scripture 33:

> 2 Thess 2:8 And then shall that Wicked be revealed, whom the Lord shall consume with the spirit of his mouth, and shall destroy with the brightness of his coming: KJV

My comment: again 2nd second coming when seen by all.

Scripture 34:

> Jer 25:33 And the slain of the Lord shall be at that day from one end of the earth even unto the other

end of the earth: they shall not be lamented, neither gathered, nor buried; they shall be dung upon the ground. KJV

My comment: Not pertinent.

Scripture 35:

> Zeph 1:2-3 I will utterly consume all things from off the land, saith the Lord. 3 I will consume man and beast; I will consume the fowls of the heaven, and the fishes of the sea, and the stumbling blocks with the wicked; and I will cut off man from off the land, saith the Lord. KJV

My comment: Not pertinent.

Scripture 36:

> Ps 110:5-6 The Lord at thy right hand shall strike through kings in the day of his wrath.
>
> 6 He shall judge among the heathen, he shall fill the places with the dead bodies; he shall wound the heads over many countries. KJV

My comment: Not pertinent.

Scripture 37:

> Jer 4:23-28 I beheld the earth, and, lo, it was without form, and void; and the heavens, and they had no light. 24 I beheld the mountains, and, lo, they trembled, and all the hills moved lightly. 25 I beheld, and, lo, there was no man, and all the birds of the heavens were fled. 26 I beheld, and, lo, the fruitful place was a wilderness, and all the cities thereof were broken down at the presence of the Lord, and by his

> fierce anger. 27 For thus hath the Lord said, The whole land shall be desolate; yet will I not make a full end.
>
> 28 For this shall the earth mourn, and the heavens above be black: because I have spoken it, I have purposed it, and will not repent, neither will I turn back from it. KJV

My comment: Not pertinent.

Scripture 38:

> Matt 24:38-42 For as in the days that were before the flood they were eating and drinking, marrying and giving in marriage, until the day that Noe entered into the ark,
>
> 39 And knew not until the flood came, and took them all away; so shall also the coming of the Son of man be. 40 Then shall two be in the field; the one shall be taken, and the other left. 41 Two women shall be grinding at the mill; the one shall be taken, and the other left. 42 Watch therefore: for ye know not what hour your Lord doth come. KJV

My comment: He says this is the scripture used by "dispensationalists" to prove the secret rapture and that no secrecy is revealed in this verse. What he does not see is that this cannot be Jesus's triumphal second second coming in power, great glory, with all the angels and a lot of noise when he does say the rapture takes place. There was no warning when the flood took place, it just happened. Here we are warned that it will be the same. In great contrast to when he says it will take place, there will be the greatest warning the earth has ever seen. Jesus's coming will be flashed like lighting from east to west. Mat 24v27 His version is a complete misreading of the verse.

Scripture 39:

> 1 John 2:18-19 Little children, it is the last time: and as ye have heard that antichrist shall come, even now are there many antichrists; whereby we know that it is the last time.
>
> 19 They went out from us, but they were not of us; for if they had been of us, they would no doubt have continued with us: but they went out, that they might be made manifest that they were not all of us. KJV

My comment: Not pertinent.

Scripture 40:

> Heb 9:27 And as it is appointed unto men once to die, but after this the judgment: KJV

My comment: Not pertinent.

Scripture 41:

> Isa 55:7 Let the wicked forsake his way, and the unrighteous man his thoughts: and let him return unto the Lord, and he will have mercy upon him; and to our God, for he will abundantly pardon. KJV

My comment: Not pertinent.

Scripture 42:

> 2 Thess 1:6-7 Seeing it is a righteous thing with God to recompense tribulation to them that trouble you; 7 And to you who are troubled rest with us, when the Lord Jesus shall be revealed from heaven with his mighty angels, KJV

My comment: Not pertinent.

Scripture 43:

> Matt 13:30 Let both grow together until the harvest: and in the time of harvest I will say to the reapers, Gather ye together first the tares, and bind them in bundles to burn them: but gather the wheat into my barn. KJV

My comment: Not pertinent.

Scripture 44:

> Rev 7:13-14 And one of the elders answered, saying unto me, What are these which are arrayed in white robes? and whence came they? 14 And I said unto him, Sir, thou knowest. And he said to me, These are they which came out of great tribulation, and have washed their robes, and made them white in the blood of the Lamb. KJV

My comment: Here he categorically states that that the saints have to go through the tribulation and are not raptured before it. He quotes his version of verse 14 as reading "these are the ones who came out of **the great tribulation**". The KJV reads "These are they which came **out of great tribulation**" and not **the great tribulation**. This difference is vitally important. In the **PROVING THE RAPTURE** section, under the heading **Which rendering is correct?** I proved conclusively that the KJV version shown just above was correct. He is saying here that they all came out of the **greatest tribulation ever** thus proving that they had to go through it, whereas I proved that they were all the saints who ever had ever suffered tribulation. Here he read the wrong bible causing a misreading of the scriptures. There is also a second confirmation that the saints **do not** go through the **greatest tribulation ever**. The following happens in sequence: Firstly, instructions are given to the angels not to hurt the earth. Rev 7:3-4: 3 "Saying, Hurt not the earth, neither the sea, nor the trees, till we have sealed the servants of our God in their foreheads. 4 And I heard the number of them which were sealed: and there were sealed an hundred and forty and four thousand of all the tribes of the children of Israel. KJV

After the 144000 Israelites are sealed in Rev 7v5-8 the saints then appear in heaven in Rev 7:14. The uncountable number of saints from all nations are now standing in white robes in heaven, who we are told, have come out of **great tribulation**. Rev 7:14

Only after this in Rev 8:2-7 are the angels given the seven trumpets to announce the coming of the seven plagues. Rev 8:2-7:

> 2 "And I saw the seven angels which stood before God; and to them were given seven trumpets.
>
> 3 And another angel came and stood at the altar, having a golden censer; and there was given unto him much incense, that he should offer it with the prayers of all saints upon the golden altar which was before the throne.
>
> 4 And the smoke of the incense, which came with the prayers of the saints, ascended up before God out of the angel's hand.
>
> 5 And the angel took the censer, and filled it with fire of the altar, and cast it into the earth: and there were voices, and thunderings, and lightnings, and an earthquake.
>
> 6 And the seven angels which had the seven trumpets prepared themselves to sound.
>
> 7 The first angel sounded, and there followed hail and fire mingled with blood, and they were cast upon the earth: and the third part of trees was burnt up, and all green grass was burnt up". KJV

So, we can see from the above that the redeemed are already in heaven before the plagues are released. This further confirms that they do not go through the **greatest tribulation ever**.

Veith also makes mention that the Israelites were not raptured when the ten plagues, plagued Egypt. This is interesting because they were protected by God in Goshen where nothing happened to then, not even the thick darkness. They did however have to put the blood of a lamb on their door posts to ward off the Death Angel from killing their first born. Here he seems to be indicating that the redeemed would also not be raptured. He overlooks that the rapture is a way of escaping the tribulation and God has many times made a way of escape for his children. In 1 Cor 10:13 the scripture indicates that God will make a way of escape so that we will not be tested beyond our endurance. "There hath no temptation taken you but such as is common to man: but God is faithful, who will not suffer you to be tempted above that ye are able; but will with the temptation also make a way to escape, that ye may be able to bear it." We can conclude therefore, that it is entire likely that he will again make a way of escape for is children from the great tribulation as he did on all these previous occasions: Israel from the great drought by the hand of Joseph in Egypt, Israel from Egypt when its army was drowned in the Red Sea, Israel from the Midianites by the hand of Gideon, Judah from Sennacherib when Ethiopia invaded his land, In 70 AD the Cristians fled Jerusalen before the siege because they were warned by prophecies to do so and more.

Scripture 45:

> Isa 25:9 And it shall be said in that day, Lo, this is our God; we have waited for him, and he will save us: this is the Lord; we have waited for him, we will be glad and rejoice in his salvation. KJV

My comment: Not pertinent.

Scripture 46:

> Matt 24, Mark 13 & Luke21. He gives this list of the Signs of his Coming from them and then discusses them:
>
> War and distress
> Earthquakes
> As in the days of Noah

> Gospel preached worldwide
> False Christs
> Signs in the sun, moon and stars

My comment: Not pertinent.

Scripture 47:

> Matt 24:2-3 "2. And Jesus said unto them, See ye not all these things? verily I say unto you, There shall not be left here one stone upon another, that shall not be thrown down.
>
> 3 And as he sat upon the mount of Olives, the disciples came unto him privately, saying, Tell us, when shall these things be? and what shall be the sign of thy coming, and of the end of the world? KJV

My comment: Discusses the burning of the temple and the collecting of the gold. Not pertinent.

Scripture 48:

> Zeph 1:14-15 The great day of the Lord is near, it is near, and hasteth greatly, even the voice of the day of the Lord: the mighty man shall cry there bitterly.
>
> 15 That day is a day of wrath, a day of trouble and distress, a day of wasteness and desolation, a day of darkness and gloominess, a day of clouds and thick darkness, KJV

My comment: He says it will not be a good day. Not pertinent.

Scripture 49:

> Luke 21:25-26 And there shall be signs in the sun, and in the moon, and in the stars; and upon the earth

> distress of nations, with perplexity; the sea and the waves roaring;
>
> 26 Men's hearts failing them for fear, and for looking after those things which are coming on the earth: for the powers of heaven shall be shaken. KJV

My comment: He says it will not be a joyful time. Not pertinent.

Scripture 50:

> Matt 24:7 For nation shall rise against nation, and kingdom against kingdom: and there shall be famines, and pestilences, and earthquakes, in divers places. KJV

My comment: Not pertinent.

Scripture 51:

> James 5:3 Your gold and silver is cankered; and the rust of them shall be a witness against you, and shall eat your flesh as it were fire. Ye have heaped treasure together for the last days. KJV

My comment: Not pertinent.

My findings on the examination of Professor Walter Veith's video debunking "The secret rapture".

1. I found that his contention that the rapture will not be secret one is correct, as all the earth will hear the voice of the archangel and hear the trumpet sound. 1 Thess 4:16 "For the Lord himself shall descend from heaven with a shout, with the voice of the archangel, and with the trump of God: and the dead in Christ shall rise first:" KJV
2. And that none of the scriptures given by him preclude the rapture happening before the Greatest Tribulation Ever.

3. I noticed that he has quoted from the NKJV (New King James Version) for most, if not all his scriptures. I seems as if he unknowingly fell in to a trap set by the translators of the **NKJV** bible when they changed the reading of Rev 7:14 in the **KJV** to "And I said to him, "Sir, you know." So he said to me, "These are the ones who come out of **the great tribulation**, and washed their robes and made them white in the blood of the Lamb." from Rev 7:14 in the **KJV** which reads "And I said unto him, Sir, thou knowest. And he said to me, These are they which came out of **great tribulation**, and have washed their robes, and made them white in the blood of the Lamb." KJV The difference is profound, in the first event only those who were in the **greatest tribulation ever** are included, and in the second event all those who were ever in **great tribulation** are included. The first rendering would have confirmed his understanding that these saints had all gone through the **greatest tribulation ever** because it said so. Only if he checked the Douay-Rheims or the Webster bibles would they have confirmed the **KJV**. The others as far as I have checked, all give the rendering as the NKJV. He is not alone as my minister believes the same. They both believe Interpretation 1 which does not add up if you think it through. If you believe Jesus comes in the clouds to the earth, uses his great power to rapture his saints, then goes and defeats the antichrist with his armies, and then with every eye watching he lands on the Mount of Olives for the marriage of the Lamb supper. The big problem with this Interpretation 1, is how do the saints get to be in heaven and also before the plagues are released?

CHAPTER 14

THE FINAL CONCLUSION OF THE EXAMINATION OF PROFESSOR WALTER VEITH'S VIDEO DEBUNKING THE SECRET RAPTURE

The conclusion is that all those with their names written in the Lamb's Book of Life are raptured and appear with the Lord in heaven before the Lord's Judgements happen on the earth. The time order from John's Revelations is the great day of the Lord's wrath in Rev 6:17, then the saints appear in heaven in Rev 7:14, and then the 7th seal is opened in Rev 8:1 announcing the coming of the final calamities.

This means he has not been able to debunk the rapture of all the believers prior to the Greatest Tribulation Ever.

Proof that Christians Do Not Die in the Coming Great Tribulation

ANNXURE 1: A COMPLETE TIME PLOT OF THE LAST DAYS EVENTS

A TIME PLOT OF THE LAST DAYS v250118

COLOUR CHART LEGEND
- PRE-LAST DAYS
- ANTICHRIST RULE BEGINS
- TRIBULATION
- MILLENNIUM
- WARS
- NEW HEAVEN AND EARTH
- LORDS RETURNS TWICE

Timeline

PRE-LAST DAYS

1260 DAYS OR 3,5 YEARS
- 7 YEAR PEACE COVENANT SIGNED WITH ISRAEL
- 2 WITNESSES, 3RD TEMPLE BUILT, THE ANTICHRIST RULES AND PERSECUTES CHRISTIANS FOR 3,5 YEARS, THE MASS FALLING AWAY, FALSE PROPHET'S MIRACLES, MARK OF THE BEAST AND SUNDAY LAW
- THE ARMAGEDDON WAR STARTS
- RAPTURE OF THE CHURCH
- JERUSALEM IS TAKEN AND THE SACRIFICE STOPPED

1335 DAYS OR 3,7 YEARS
- ERECTION OF ABOMINATION OF DESOLATION IDOL
- THE ARMAGEDDON WAR CONTINUES, THE GREATEST TRIBULATION EVER BEGINS IMMEDATELY WITH AN EARTHQUAKE IN JERUSALEM AND THE JUDGEMENTS CONTINUE FOR 3,5 YEARS
- THE LORD RETURNS WITH THE SAINTS AND STANDS ON THE MOUNT OF OLIVES
- BEAST AND FALSE PROPHET CAST IN TO THE LAKE OF FIRE

1000 YEARS
- SATAN BOUND FOR 1000 YEARS
- THE 1000 YEAR MILLENNIUM

- SATAN RELEASED
- THE GOG & MAGOG WAR
- SATAN CAST IN TO THE LAKE OF FIRE
- GREAT WHITE THRONE JUDGEMENT
- A NEW HEAVEN AND NEW EARTH AND THE NEW JERUSALEM

Daniel Heynike

ANNXURE 2: A COMPLETE TIME PLOT OF THE EVENTS IN REVELATION 12

A TIME PLOT OF REV 12 v250118

EVENTS ON THE EARTH

Antichrist in authority Dan 9v27

- Rev 11v3 The two witnesses prophesy for 1260 days (3.5YRS)
- Rev 13v13 The false prophet brings down fire from heaven
- Rev 13v17 Cannot trade without the mark or name of the beast
- SUNDAY LAW INFORCE Annexure 3
- THIRD TEMPLE BEING BUILT IN JERUSALEM
- 1260 DAYS OR 3.5 YEARS
- 7 YEAR PEACE COVENANT SIGNED WITH ISRAEL Dan 9:27

RAPTURE OCCURS HERE > >

JERUSALEM IS CONQUERED AND THE DAILY SACRIFICE STOPPED

ERRECTION OF THE IDOL OF ABOMINATION AND DESOLATION

Antichrist in authority Dan 9v27

- Rev 12:10-12: Christ's Kingdom comes as Jesus revokes the authority Satan obtained from Adam when he sinned causing rejoicing by all the saints and angels in heaven
- Rev 12v9: Satan cast out of heaven to the earth
- Dan 12:12: Blessed is he that cometh to the 1335 days
- Dan12v11: after the abomination is set up, there shall be 1290 days
- Rev 12v6: Jews sheltered and fed for 1260 days (3.5YRS)
- Rev 19-20 fire comes down on those with the mark of the beast
- JERUSALEM WAR JUST BEFORE THE LORD RETURNS: ZECH 14 then ARMAGEDDON

JUDGEMENT AND THE GREATEST TRIBULATION EVER BEGINS WITH AN EARTHQUAKE IMMEDIATELY AFTER THE ERRECTION OF THE ABOMINATION THAT CAUSES DESOLATION IDOL

THE LORD RETURNS   Zechariah 14v4

BEAST AND FALSE PROPHET CAST INTO THE LAKE OF FIRE Rev 19:20

EVENTS IN HEAVEN

RAPTURED SAINTS APPEAR IN HEAVEN Rev 7:9 After this I beheld, and, lo, a great multitude, which no man could number, of all nations, and kindreds, and people, and tongues, stood before the throne, and before the Lamb, clothed with white robes, and palms in their hands. MARRIAGE SUPPER OF THE LAMB Rev 19:7

88

ANNEXURE 3: THE ARK OF THE COVENANT

This is my recollection and comments on a 1.5-hour video I watched of the discovery of the Ark of the Covenant. The video is on YouTube where you can view all Ron Wyatt's discovery movies, just search for "ron wyatt". The title you want to watch is called the "Original Ron Wyatt Ark of the Covenant Found".

The Ark was found in small cavern at the end of a long tunnel from Jeremiah's grotto in Jerusalem to a cliff face called the "Place of the Skull". Ron Wyatt was at the cliff face in the Garden Tomb area close to the place called the "Place of the Skull" in about 1978 when his arm rose up of its own accord and pointed to the cliff face and his own voice announced "that is where the Ark of the Covenant is". He was mystified by this and started researching to find if it could be true. After getting the required permissions he looked for a route from Jeremiah's grotto and other excavations in the area to the point he was shown but found route, so he decided to excavate at the point he was shown. Discovering that the current ground level was much higher than it was 2000 years ago due to filling and dumping, he excavated vertically downward next to the cliff face. During his many years of excavating, he came to a square post hole chiselled into the rock with a crack running across it, a square stone plug in it and a cave nearby. There were many interconnected caves of all sizes leading from the first cave. Some of the connections were too small for the large man that Rob was, to enter so he hired a very small local man to enter them and tell him what was inside. They eventually reached a small cave with a large single stalactite hanging from the ceiling next to the cave wall. When Ron broke it off it revealed a very small hole behind it. Shinning his torch into the hole revealed a cave filled with rocks almost to the ceiling. It did not look promising but they widened the hole to let his helper crawl in. He soon came out shouting "what's in there ", said that he was not going back, disappeared and was not seen again. Ron then widened the hole so he could get in and crawling over the stones he shone his torch downwards and saw the glint of gold.

 They re-entered the cave several times, removing stones and coverings, to reveal the table of Show Bread, the Altar of Incense, the Golden Candle Sticks and against the wall, the Ark of the Covenant. Ron knew that there had to be an entrance to the cave through which these items had been brought in but could not find it. There was dry blood on the mercy seat and immediately above it a crack in the cave ceiling, also with dry blood on it. I do not know what Ron's occupation was but I know he worked in a hospital and knew all about blood. He took a sample of the dry blood from the mercy seat to an Israeli laboratory to be analysed. The Lab rehydrated the blood and reported the following results: The blood was still alive and that there were only 24 chromosomes plus a non-human y chromosome. Ron believed the 24 belonged to his mother and the single Y to his father. The last time Ron went back they took a video camera with them but the resulting video was compromised by God's glory emanating from the Ark. When they re-entered the chamber, it was cleared of all the stones including the now visible entrance tunnel, the end of which was still blocked by stones. Four human looking angels dressed in identical non-descriptive clothes were posted at the 4 corners of the ark and the furniture had been rearranged in their correct positions. One of the angels asked Ron to video the room and the two stone 10 commandment tablets. The solid gold lid of the ark was too heavy for Ron to lift so the angels lifted it, he took the tablets out and handed them back to the angel who put them on a ledge so they could be filmed. The angel then informed Ron that the stone tablets would only be revealed when the Sunday Law was enacted. Ron in his lectures apparently made contradictory versions of what the angel had said so they asked him on his death bed what he angel really said. He replied "the Sunday Law".

BOOKS BY THE SAME AUTHOR

1. THE GREAT END TIME DECEPTION EXPOSED

A TIME ORDERED SUMMARY OF MY FINDINGS FROM MY FIRST BOOK "THE GREAT END TIME DECEPTION EXPOSED"

1. A period of great Christian tribulation has existed from the time John the Baptist had his head removed and will increase in frequency as we get closer to the end of the age, due both to the population increase, and the increase in lawlessness. There will be no end of Christian tribulation till the 'END OF THE AGE' rapture occurs.
2. The Antichrist will agree a 7 year peace treaty with Israel which will allow the Israelis to build the 3rd temple or at least Moses' Tent of Meeting.
3. In the middle of this 7 year period the Antichrist will cancel the agreement and place the abomination of desolation idol in the Jewish temple. (Matt 24:15: "stand in the holy place").
4. This is the sign of the 'END OF THE AGE' and causes an immediate reaction from God. This is where Jesus says to his disciples in Matt 24:17 that they will not even have time to fetch their clothes in their house before God's wrath is poured out on Jerusalem and Judea.
5. It is the time of the final judgement when the wrath of God is poured out on the earth and is also the time of the

RAPTURE. We know however, that the RAPTURE will precede the END TIME SIGNS of the judgement to come on all the earth because we know that when Jesus appears in the sky to collect his elect (the saints) he comes like a thief in the night. (Luke 12:40)

6. The GREATEST GLOBAL TRIBULATION EVER begins with the appearance of the abomination of desolation idol in the holy place of the Jewish temple.
7. The end of the GREATEST GLOBAL TRIBULATION EVER comes after about 3.5 years, but the precise end time is not clear. We know that God has shortened this period because otherwise no one would have survived (Matt 24:22) and we are told in Dan 12:11 that a time of 1290 days (43 months) will be counted after the start of The GREATEST GLOBAL TRIBULATION EVER begins. While this looks to be the end, verse 12 seems to contradict this saying that those who "wait" (survive) till the 1335th day (a further 45 days) will count themselves blessed.
8. After the end of the GREATEST TRIBULATION EVER the signs of the Lord's second coming are displayed and then he appears in the sky and the millennium, the 1000 years of peace on earth begins. Matt 24v 29: says "Immediately after the tribulation of those days shall the sun be darkened, and the moon shall not give her light, and the stars shall fall from heaven, and the powers of the heavens shall be shaken: 30: And then shall appear the sign of the Son of man in heaven: and then shall all the tribes of the earth mourn, and they shall see the Son of man coming in the clouds of heaven with power and great glory."
9. THE 7 YEAR END TIME TRIBULATION preached by many does not exist in the Bible.

2. REVELATIONS

Book 1: An easy-to-read and understand explanation of the revelation given to John.

Book 2: A derivation of the time lines of all the last days events. There is a lot of controversy with respect to the time of the rapture event, even among the theologians. Few have managed to correctly work it out and even fewer of those who have, are brave enough to preach on it. The author has managed to place all the end time events in the time order of each event, including the rapture (not date and time) and has included all the scriptures used to established this. This is now made available in this book for all. It is his hope that this book will inform Christians of the true situation, bring the controversy to an end, and better prepare them for the perilous times to come.

ADDENDUM: WHO IS GOING TO HEAVEN AND HOW TO MAKE SURE THAT YOU ESCAPE THE GREATEST TRIBULATION EVER AND JOIN JESUS IN HEAVEN

Not everyone is going to heaven. Revelation 21 verses 6 to 8 says the following:

> "6 And he said unto me, It is done. I am Alpha and Omega, the beginning and the end. I will give unto him that is athirst of the fountain of the water of life freely.
>
> 7 He that overcometh shall inherit all things; and I will be his God, and he shall be my son.
>
> 8 But the fearful, and unbelieving, and the abominable, and murderers, and whoremongers, and sorcerers, and idolaters, and all liars, shall have their part in the lake which burneth with fire and brimstone: which is the second death."

We see from verse 7 that we have to do something to inherit the kingdom of Heaven, we have to overcome. And what do we have to overcome? We have to overcome any or all the things mentioned in verse 8 which means that if we have just once given in to fear or unbelief, never mind the rest, we are already disqualified. This makes it impossible for anyone to get in by their own effort but not for God. You see that already in verse 7, the verse that says you have to overcome, it is already pointing to Gods solution by saying that you **inherit** the kingdom of Heaven. In other words you can't earn it, you get it because of your relationship with your father. We can now explain that the things in verse 8 that keep you out of heaven are Satanic and not acceptable in heaven. Jesus is simply telling you that you have to be a lover of God and hater of Satan to be acceptable in heaven. Here we must not lose heart because God has a magnificent plan for our salvation and it is called JESUS and he wrote these words to us in John 3 verses 16 & 17:

> "For God so loved the world, that he gave his only begotten Son, that whosoever believeth in him should not perish, but have everlasting life. For God sent not his Son into the world to condemn the world; but that the world through him might be saved."

So, we can confirm that God wants you in Heaven, so how do you get there? Fortunately, he also shows us the way.

The way of salvation

Firstly, you need to decide that you want to be with Jesus in Heaven.

Secondly, you need to decide that you do not want to serve Satan any more but be righteous even as Jesus is righteous in Heaven.

You can achieve this because the scriptures declare in John 1 verses 8 to 9:

> "8 If we say that we have no sin, we deceive ourselves, and the truth is not in us.
>
> 9 If we confess our sins, he is faithful and just to forgive us our sins, and to cleanse us from all unrighteousness."

Also, the word says in Romans 10 verses 8-10

> "8 But what saith it? The word is nigh thee, even in thy mouth, and in thy heart: that is, the word of faith, which we preach;
>
> 9 That if thou shalt confess with thy mouth the Lord Jesus, and shalt believe in thine heart that God hath raised him from the dead, thou shalt be saved.
>
> 10 For with the heart man believeth unto righteousness; and with the mouth confession is made unto salvation."

So, if you confess to Jesus that you have sinned and you also confess that he is Lord of your life you will be saved. Now all you have to do is pray the prayer below aloud and mean it and salvation is yours.

Sinners' prayer (say aloud)

DEAR LORD JESUS I ACKNOWLEDGE THAT I HAVE SINNED AND ASK YOU TO FORGIVE ALL MY SINS, PAST, PRESENT AND FUTURE. I ASK YOU TO BE MY LORD AND SAVOUR AND LIVE WITH ME FOREVER MORE.

If you have said this prayer, I welcome you into the body of Christ. All the angels in heaven are rejoicing over your salvation. You are however still a baby in Christ and will need good food to grow strong. Please read the next section "How to become a strong Christian".

How to become a strong Christian

Do the following. The order of importance is from top to bottom.
1. Get a bible. I only quote from the King James Version (also called authorised version, best if you can understand it), or New King James (2nd best) or American Standard Version.
2. Read and study it every day.
3. Find a church that believes Jesus is God and believes in baptism in water and also baptism in the Holy Spirit.

4. Join a bible study group.
5. Get baptised in water.
6. Get baptised in the Holy Spirit.
7. Get a concordance. A Crudence paper back will do.
8. Get a commentary. A Hodder Bible Handbook or similar will do but read your bible and study it before using the hand book.

www.ingramcontent.com/pod-product-compliance
Lightning Source LLC
LaVergne TN
LVHW061625070526
838199LV00070B/6578